MW01168637

365 DAILY DEVOTIONAL FOR FOR MILITARY PERSONNEL

BY

DOVE PUBLICATION

Copyright© 2023 Dove Publication

All Rights Reserved.

DEDICATON

I Dedicate This Book to Almighty God. And People That Assisted Me One Way or The Other, God Bless You All Richly.

INTRODUTION

Have you ever stared up at a star-strewn sky, rifle heavy in your hands, and felt a sliver of doubt pierce the steely resolve in your chest? Or knelt in the mud of a foreign land, the weight of the world pressing down, and longed for a whisper of hope amidst the chaos? Soldier, you are not alone.

This devotional isn't just another dusty manual collecting grit in your pack. It's a lifeline, a spark to ignite the fire within. It's for the moments when fatigue threatens to extinguish your spirit, when the weight of duty feels like an iron burden. It's for the quiet watches, the camaraderie forged in shared hardship, and the yearning for home that aches with every sunrise.

Within these pages, you'll find solace in the testaments of those who walked the path before you. Warriors of faith, etched in the annals of history, who faced darkness with unwavering courage, their hearts anchored in something greater than the battlefield. You'll discover the unwavering strength that resides not just in your training and weaponry, but in the wellspring of faith that resides within.

This is a wellspring that transcends religious boundaries. It's about the quiet strength that gets you through the long patrol, the unwavering loyalty that binds you to your brothers and sisters in arms, and the unwavering hope that carries you through the bleakest night. It's about finding purpose in the face of uncertainty, and clinging to the belief that what you do matters.

Here, you'll find meditations crafted with the grit of the battlefield in mind. No flowery prose, no sugar-coating the harsh realities you face. These are words born from the shared experiences of those who've served, who understand the language of sacrifice and the weight of responsibility.

But this journey isn't just about weathering the storm. It's about finding pockets of light within the darkness. It's about celebrating the resilience of the human spirit, the unbreakable bonds forged in the crucible of conflict, and the unwavering love that carries you home. It's about finding moments of peace amidst the chaos, of gratitude for the simple things, and the unwavering hope for a brighter future.

So, soldier, take a deep breath. Let this devotional be your compass, a guiding star in the darkest night. Let it be your solace, your source of strength, and a constant reminder that you are not alone. You carry the weight of the world, yes, but you also carry the unwavering spirit that will see you through. Open these pages, and let the journey begin.

But under the stoic exterior, a human heart beat. It yearns for home, for the comfort of loved ones left behind. It wrestles with fear, with the uncertainty that hangs heavy in the air. It grapples with the weight of decisions, with the knowledge that every action might have life-altering consequences.

May this journey of devotion be a source of comfort and inspiration. May it remind you of the unwavering love that surrounds you, and the profound purpose that drives you. Amen.

DAY 1
THE ARMOR OF FAITH

Scripture: "Finally, my brethren, be strong in the Lord, and in the power of his might. Put on the whole armour of God, that ye may be able to stand against the wiles of the devil." - Ephesians 6:10-11 (KJV)

Just as a soldier prepares for battle by putting on armor, so too must you prepare for the spiritual battles you face. Ephesians reminds us that our strength comes from the Lord, and we are called to put on the whole armor of God to stand against the schemes of the enemy. Each piece of the armor – the belt of truth, the breastplate of righteousness, the shoes of peace, the shield of faith, the helmet of salvation, and the sword of the Spirit – equips us for spiritual warfare. With faith as our shield and the Word of God as our sword, we can boldly face the challenges ahead, knowing that God fights alongside us.

Prayer: Heavenly Father, thank You for the armor You provide to equip me for spiritual battle. Help me to put on the whole armor of God each day, that I may stand firm against the enemy's attacks. Strengthen our faith and empower me to walk in Your truth. In Jesus' name, amen.

DAY 2
COURAGE UNDER FIRE

Scripture: "Have not I commanded thee? Be strong and of a good courage; be not afraid, neither be thou dismayed: for the Lord thy God is with thee whithersoever thou goest." - Joshua 1:9 (KJV)

In the face of adversity, God commands us to be strong and courageous, for He is always with us. Joshua, as he prepared to lead the Israelites into the promised land, received this assurance from the Lord: "Be strong and of a good courage; be not afraid." Like Joshua, you may face daunting challenges and uncertain circumstances, but you can take courage in knowing that the Lord your God goes with you wherever you go. His presence is your source of strength and courage, enabling you to persevere through the trials and tribulations of life.

Prayer: Gracious God, thank You for Your promise to be with me wherever I go. Grant me the courage and strength to face the challenges ahead, knowing that You are always by my side. Help me to trust in Your unfailing love and find courage in Your presence. In Jesus' name, amen.

DAY 3
DISCIPLINE OF THE SPIRIT

Scripture: "For God hath not given us the spirit of fear; but of power, and of love, and of a sound mind." - 2 Timothy 1:7 (KJV)

God has given us a spirit of power, love, and self-discipline, enabling us to overcome fear and live boldly for Him. In times of uncertainty or struggle, we can rely on the strength of the Holy Spirit within us to guide and empower us. Through prayer, meditation on God's Word, and obedience to His commands, we cultivate the discipline of the spirit, allowing us to live with confidence and purpose. Instead of succumbing to fear or doubt, we can trust in God's provision and walk in the freedom He has given us.

Prayer: Heavenly Father, thank You for the spirit of power, love, and self-discipline You have given me. Help me to cultivate discipline in my live, that I may walk in confidence and obedience to Your will. Fill me afresh with Your Holy Spirit, empowering me to live boldly for Your glory. In Jesus' name, amen.

DAY 4
LEADERSHIP WITH WISDOM

Scripture: "By me kings reign, and princes decree justice. By me princes' rule, and nobles, even all the judges of the earth." - Proverbs 8:15-16 (KJV)

True leadership is rooted in wisdom, which comes from God alone. Proverbs teaches us that kings reign and princes rule by wisdom, and it is through wisdom that justice is established and righteousness upheld. As you step into positions of leadership, whether in your family, workplace, or community, seek after God's wisdom above all else. Let His Word be your guide and His Spirit your counselor, as you make decisions and lead others with integrity and humility.

Prayer: Gracious God, we thank You for the wisdom You provide to guide us in leadership. Grant us discernment and understanding as we navigate the responsibilities entrusted to us. May Your wisdom be evident in all our decisions and actions, bringing glory to Your name. In Jesus' name, amen.

DAY 5
THE SOLDIER'S PSALM

Scripture: "He that dwelleth in the secret place of the most High shall abide under the shadow of the Almighty. I will say of the Lord, He is my refuge and my fortress: my God; in him will I trust." - Psalm 91:1-2 (KJV)

Psalm 91 is often called the soldier's psalm, as it offers comfort and protection to those facing danger or hardship. It reminds us that when we dwell in the secret place of the Most High, we find refuge and strength in His presence. As you journey through life's battles, take comfort in knowing that the Lord is your refuge and fortress. He is your shield and protector, guarding you from harm and preserving you in times of trouble. Trust in His promises and rest securely in His care, for He is faithful to deliver and sustain His children.

Prayer: Heavenly Father, thank You for being our refuge and fortress, our ever-present help in times of trouble. Grant us the faith to trust in Your protection and the courage to face whatever challenges come our way. May we dwell in Your presence and find peace in Your sheltering arms. In Jesus' name, amen.

DAY 6
MARCHING ORDERS FROM ABOVE

Scripture: "Thy word is a lamp unto my feet, and a light unto my path." - Psalm 119:105 (KJV)

As military personnel, your path is often shrouded in uncertainty. But fear not, for God's word serves as your guiding light, illuminating the way forward. Just as soldiers diligently follow their orders, so too must you heed the commands of your heavenly Commander.

In the quiet moments of prayer and reflection, listen for His voice. His directives may come in the form of a still, small whisper or a powerful conviction in your heart. Whatever the method, trust that His guidance is sure and true.

Let the Word of God be your compass, leading you through the trials and triumphs of military life. With each step, march boldly forward, knowing that you are not alone. The Almighty marches alongside you, ever faithful and ever true.

Prayer: Almighty God, thank You for Your guiding light that leads me on the path of righteousness. Grant me the wisdom to discern Your marching orders and the courage to follow them faithfully. In Your holy name, Amen.

DAY 7
STRENGTH IN THE TRENCHES

Scripture: "I can do all things through Christ which strengtheneth me." - Philippians 4:13 (KJV)

In the trenches of life, when the battles rage fierce and the burdens seem unbearable, remember that your strength comes from the Lord. Just as soldiers rely on their training and camaraderie in the heat of combat, so too can you draw upon the power of Christ within you.

When fatigue sets in and doubts assail your mind, cling to the promises of God's Word. He promises to uphold you with His righteous right hand and to renew your strength like the eagle's.

No matter the trials you face, take heart knowing that you are not fighting alone. The Lord of hosts is by your side, empowering you to overcome every obstacle in your path.

Prayer: Heavenly Father, strengthen me with Your mighty hand as I face the challenges of each day. Help me to find courage and perseverance in Your unfailing love. In Jesus' name, Amen.

DAY 8
VALOR IN QUIET MOMENTS

Scripture: "Be still, and know that I am God..." - Psalm 46:10
(KJV)

In the midst of the chaos and clamor of military life, carve out moments of quietude to commune with your Creator. True valor is not only found on the battlefield but also in the stillness of your soul as you surrender to God's will. As you lay down your weapons of worry and anxiety, allow His peace to envelop you like a warm embrace. In the silence, you will find strength to face the challenges ahead and clarity to discern His purpose for your life.

Embrace these moments of solitude as opportunities for spiritual renewal and restoration. For it is in the quiet moments that God speaks most clearly, guiding you with His gentle voice and filling you with His perfect peace.

Prayer: Gracious God, grant me the courage to be still and trust in Your sovereignty. May Your peace reign in my heart as I rest in Your presence. Amen.

DAY 9
COMMANDING PEACE

Scripture: "And the peace of God, which passeth all understanding, shall keep your hearts and minds through Christ Jesus." - Philippians 4:7 (KJV)

In the midst of chaos and conflict, you have the power to command peace. Not through force of arms, but through the authority of Christ dwelling within you. Just as a commanding officer brings order to the ranks, so too can you bring calm to the stormy seas of life. Speak peace over every situation, trusting in the promise of God's Word to guard your heart and mind. When fear and anxiety threaten to overwhelm you, declare His peace that surpasses all understanding.

As you walk in obedience to His commands, His peace will become a fortress around you, shielding you from the arrows of doubt and despair. Stand firm in the authority He has given you, knowing that nothing can stand against the peace of God that reigns within you.

Prayer: Prince of Peace, I command Your peace to rule and reign in every area of my life. Let Your tranquility guards my heart and mind, even in the midst of turmoil. Amen.

DAY 10
THE WARRIOR'S INTEGRITY

Scripture: "The integrity of the upright shall guide them..." - Proverbs 11:3 (KJV)

As a warrior, your integrity is your greatest weapon. It is the steadfastness of character that inspires trust and commands respect, both on and off the battlefield. Just as a well-forged sword is tested in the heat of combat, so too will your integrity be proven in the crucible of adversity. Let your actions be guided by the moral compass of God's Word, standing firm in righteousness and truth. Uphold the values of honor, courage, and selflessness, knowing that you represent something greater than yourself.

In a world that often values expedience over integrity, be a beacon of light shining brightly in the darkness. Let your integrity be a testimony to the transforming power of Christ within you, drawing others to Him through your example.

Prayer: Lord, grant me the strength to uphold my integrity in all circumstances. May my words and deeds reflect Your righteousness and bring glory to Your name. Amen.

DAY 11
TACTICAL PATIENCE

Scripture: "But let patience have her perfect work, that ye may be perfect and entire, wanting nothing." - James 1:4 (KJV)

In the heat of battle, tactical patience is your ally. Just as a skilled strategist waits for the opportune moment to strike, so too must you exercise patience in the midst of adversity. Trust in the Lord's timing, for He knows the beginning from the end. As you wait upon Him, remember the example of Abraham, who patiently waited for the fulfilment of God's promises. His faith was counted unto him for righteousness, and he became the father of many nations. Embrace patience as a virtue to be cultivated, knowing that it produces endurance and strengthens your character. May your heart be steadfast, trusting in the Lord's faithfulness to bring victory in His perfect time.

Prayer: Heavenly Father, grant me the grace to wait patiently upon You, knowing that Your timing is perfect. Help me to trust in Your promises and to rest in Your unfailing love. Amen.

DAY 12
STRATEGIC PRAYERS FOR BATTLE

Scripture: "Pray without ceasing." - 1 Thessalonians 5:17 (KJV)

In the battlefield of life, prayer is your most powerful weapon. Just as a skilled general devises strategic plan for victory, so too must you engage in strategic prayers for battle. Let your petitions be guided by the wisdom of God's Word and the leading of His Spirit. Pray not only for your own strength and protection but also for your fellow soldiers in the faith. Lift up one another in prayer, knowing that the fervent prayers of the righteous avail much.

Take authority over the enemy through prayer, declaring victory in the name of Jesus. For greater is He that is in you than he that is in the world.

Prayer: Mighty God, teach me to pray strategically, according to Your will. Grant me discernment to know how to pray and faith to believe for victory in every battle. Amen.

DAY 13
CAMARADERIE IN CHRIST

Scripture: "A friend loveth at all times, and a brother is born for adversity." - Proverbs 17:17 (KJV)

In the fellowship of believers, you find camaraderie in Christ. Just as soldiers stand shoulder to shoulder in the face of danger, so too do you stand united with your brothers and sisters in the faith. Encourage one another, bearing each other's burdens and lifting one another up in prayer. For where two or three are gathered together in His name, there He is in the midst of them.

Let love be the hallmark of your relationships, reflecting the love of Christ that binds you together. May your unity in Him be a powerful testimony to the world of His saving grace.

Prayer: Loving Father, thank You for the gift of spiritual family. Help me to cherish and nurture the bonds of fellowship with my brothers and sisters in Christ. May our love for one another be a reflection of Your love for us. Amen.

DAY 14
THE GENERAL'S HUMILITY

Scripture: "He hath shewed thee, O man, what is good; and what doth the Lord require of thee, but to do justly, and to love mercy, and to walk humbly with thy God?" - Micah 6:8 (KJV)

In the hierarchy of the military, humility is often seen as a weakness. But in the kingdom of God, it is a mark of true greatness. Follow the example of Jesus, who humbled Himself and took on the form of a servant. As a leader, lead with humility, recognizing that all authority comes from God. Serve your subordinates with compassion and grace, knowing that you too are under authority.

Walk humbly before the Lord, acknowledging your dependence on Him for wisdom and strength. May your life be a living testimony to the transforming power of His grace.

Prayer: Gracious Father, teach me to walk humbly before You and others. May Your humility be reflected in my words and actions, that You may be glorified in all that I do. Amen.

DAY 15
THE SHIELD OF PERSEVERANCE

Scripture: "And let us not be weary in well doing: for in due season we shall reap, if we faint not." - Galatians 6:9 (KJV)

In the midst of trials and tribulations, perseverance is your shield. Just as a soldier withstands the onslaught of the enemy with his shield, so too must you stand firm in the face of adversity. Do not grow weary in doing good, for in due season you will reap a harvest if you do not give up. Take heart in the promises of God's Word, knowing that He who has called you is faithful.

Press on toward the goal, fixing your eyes on Jesus, the author and perfecter of your faith. For He has overcome the world, and in Him, you are more than conquerors.

Prayer: Heavenly Father, strengthen me with Your power to persevere in the midst of trials. Help me to stand firm in faith, knowing that You are with me always. Amen.

DAY 16
RECONNAISSANCE OF THE HEART

Scripture: "Search me, O God, and know my heart: try me, and know my thoughts." - Psalm 139:23 (KJV)

In the midst of the battlefield, don't forget to conduct reconnaissance of your heart. Just as a skilled soldier surveys the terrain for hidden dangers, so too must you examine your innermost thoughts and motives. Allow the light of God's Word to penetrate the depths of your soul, revealing any areas of darkness or deceit. Surrender your heart to Him completely, trusting that He alone can purify and cleanse it. As you submit to His inspection, He will lead you in the paths of righteousness and truth. Let your heart be a sanctuary for His presence, a dwelling place for His Spirit to abide.

Prayer: Gracious Father, search my heart and reveal anything that is not pleasing in Your sight. Purify me, O Lord, and make me whole. May my heart be a pleasing sacrifice unto You. Amen.

DAY 17
THE BATTLE PLAN OF PURITY

Scripture: "Blessed are the pure in heart: for they shall see God." - Matthew 5:8 (KJV)

In the heat of spiritual warfare, purity is your battle plan. Just as a soldier prepares for battle by cleansing and sharpening his weapons, so too must you purify your heart and mind. Guard your eyes and ears from the defilement of sin, filling your thoughts with whatever is true, noble, and pure. Clothe yourself in the armor of righteousness, standing firm against the schemes of the enemy.

Strive for purity in all areas of your life, knowing that those who are pure in heart will see God. Let your thoughts and actions be pleasing in His sight, reflecting the purity of His holiness.

Prayer: Holy God, create in me a clean heart and renew a right spirit within me. Help me to walk in purity and holiness, that I may see You and glorify Your name. Amen.

DAY 18

THE FELLOWSHIP OF THE BRAVE

Scripture: "Be strong and of a good courage, fear not, nor be afraid of them: for the Lord thy God, he it is that doth go with thee; he will not fail thee, nor forsake thee." - Deuteronomy 31:6 (KJV)

In the fellowship of the brave, you find strength and courage to face the battles ahead. Just as soldiers stand united on the battlefield, so too must you stand shoulder to shoulder with your brothers and sisters in Christ. Encourage one another in the faith, lifting each other up in prayer and support. For where two or three are gathered together in His name, there He is in the midst of them.

Take heart in the promises of God's Word, knowing that He will never leave you nor forsake you. Let your fellowship be a source of strength and encouragement, as you press on toward the goal together.

Prayer: Mighty God, thank You for the fellowship of believers. Strengthen our bonds of unity and empower us to stand firm in the face of adversity. May Your presence be ever with us as we journey together in faith. Amen.

DAY 19
THE TACTICAL ADVANTAGE OF FORGIVENESS

Scripture: "And be ye kind one to another, tender-hearted, forgiving one another, even as God for Christ's sake hath forgiven you." - Ephesians 4:32 (KJV)

In the midst of conflict, forgiveness is your tactical advantage. Just as a skilled general seeks to reconcile with his enemies, so too must you extend forgiveness to those who have wronged you. Forgiveness is not a sign of weakness, but of strength. It releases you from the chains of bitterness and resentment, freeing you to experience the fullness of God's grace.

Follow the example of Christ, who forgave those who crucified Him, saying, "Father, forgive them, for they know not what they do." Let your heart be filled with His love and compassion, extending forgiveness to all who have hurt you.

Prayer: Merciful Father, teach me to forgive as You have forgiven me. Grant me the strength to release the hurts of the past and to walk in the freedom of Your grace. Amen.

DAY 20
THE MISSION OF MERCY

Scripture: "He hath shewed thee, O man, what is good; and what doth the Lord require of thee, but to do justly, and to love mercy, and to walk humbly with thy God?" - Micah 6:8 (KJV)

In the mission of mercy, you demonstrate the love of Christ to a hurting world. Just as a compassionate medic tends to the wounded on the battlefield, so too must you extend mercy and compassion to those in need. Seek justice for the oppressed and marginalized, showing kindness and mercy to all. For blessed are the merciful, for they shall obtain mercy.

Let your life be a living testimony to the transformative power of God's love and grace. May your acts of mercy shine brightly in the darkness, drawing others to the hope found in Christ alone.

Prayer: Compassionate Father, fill me with Your love and mercy, that I may be a beacon of hope to those in need. Use me to bring healing and restoration to a broken world, for Your glory and honor. Amen.

DAY 21
THE STRATEGY OF GIVING

Scripture: "Give, and it shall be given unto you; good measure, pressed down, and shaken together, and running over, shall men give into your bosom. For with the same measure that ye mete withal it shall be measured to you again." - Luke 6:38 (KJV)

In the strategy of giving, you unlock the abundant blessings of God. Just as a wise commander invests resources strategically for victory, so too must you give generously and cheerfully, trusting in God's provision. Follow the example of Jesus, who gave His life as a ransom for many. Give not out of compulsion or obligation, but out of a heart overflowing with gratitude for all that God has done for you.

As you sow seeds of generosity, God promises to multiply your harvest, blessing you abundantly beyond measure. Let your giving be a reflection of His love and generosity, shining brightly in a world in need of hope.

Prayer: Heavenly Father, teach me the joy of giving sacrificially and cheerfully. May my generosity be a testimony to Your abundant provision and grace. Amen.

DAY 22
THE ART OF WAR AND PEACE

Scripture: "Blessed are the peacemakers: for they shall be called the children of God." - Matthew 5:9 (KJV)

In the art of war and peace, you are called to be a peacemaker. Just as a skilled diplomat seeks to resolve conflicts peacefully, so too must you strive to bring harmony and reconciliation in all areas of your life. Follow the example of Jesus, who came to bring peace between God and man through His sacrifice on the cross. Pursue peace with all people, even in the midst of conflict and strife.

Be quick to listen, slow to speak, and slow to anger, seeking to understand the perspectives of others with empathy and compassion. For blessed are the peacemakers, for they shall be called the children of God.

Prayer: Prince of Peace, grant me the wisdom and grace to be a peacemaker in a world filled with strife and division. Help me to reflect Your love and reconciliation in all that I do. Amen.

DAY 23
THE SENTINEL'S WATCH

Scripture: "Watch ye, stand fast in the faith, quit you like men, be strong." - 1 Corinthians 16:13 (KJV)

As a sentinel on the watchtower, you must remain vigilant and alert. Just as a watchman scans the horizon for signs of danger, so too must you guard your heart and mind against the schemes of the enemy. Be sober-minded and alert, for your adversary the devil prowls around like a roaring lion, seeking whom he may devour. Put on the full armor of God, standing firm in the faith and resisting the attacks of the evil one.

Prayer: Almighty God, help me to be vigilant and alert, standing firm in the faith and resisting the attacks of the enemy. Grant me the strength and courage to be a faithful sentinel on the watchtower. Amen.

DAY 24
THE WARRIOR'S REST

Scripture: "Come unto me, all ye that labour and are heavy laden, and I will give you rest." - Matthew 11:28 (KJV)

In the midst of battle, find rest in the presence of the Lord. Just as a weary soldier seeks refuge and reprieve from the heat of the day, so too must you come to Jesus and find rest for your soul. Cast your cares upon Him, for He cares for you. Lay down your burdens at His feet and take up His yoke, for His burden is light and His yoke is easy.

Prayer: Gracious Father, thank You for the rest that You provide for my soul. Help me to find refuge and reprieve in Your presence, and to trust in Your unfailing love. Amen.

DAY 25
THE HIGH GROUND OF HOPE

Scripture: "Why art thou cast down, O my soul? and why art thou disquieted in me? hope thou in God: for I shall yet praise him for the help of his countenance." - Psalm 42:5 (KJV)

In the midst of adversity, take refuge in the high ground of hope. Just as a soldier gains a strategic advantage by occupying the high ground, so too must you lift your eyes to the hills from whence comes your help. Anchor your hope in the promises of God's Word, knowing that He is faithful and true. Though the storms may rage and the battles may rage, trust in the Lord with all your heart, and lean not on your own understanding.

Prayer: Sovereign Lord, help me to anchor my hope in You alone, knowing that You are my strength and my salvation. May Your unfailing love sustain me through every trial and tribulation. Amen.

DAY 26
THE SOLDIER'S SACRIFICE

Scripture: "Greater love hath no man than this, that a man lay down his life for his friends." - John 15:13 (KJV)

The soldier's sacrifice embodies the essence of selflessness and love. Just as Jesus laid down His life for us, so too must you be willing to sacrifice for the greater good. Reflect on the ultimate sacrifice of Christ on the cross, where He bore the weight of our sins and gave His life to redeem us. Let His example inspire you to lay down your own desires and ambitions for the sake of others.

Embrace sacrificial living, giving of your time, talents, and resources to serve those in need. For in giving, you receive the abundant blessings of God's grace and provision.

Prayer: Loving Father, grant me the courage to sacrifice for the sake of others, following the example of Your Son, Jesus Christ. Help me to embody the selfless love that He demonstrated on the cross. Amen.

DAY 27
THE CADENCE OF UNITY

Scripture: "Behold, how good and how pleasant it is for brethren to dwell together in unity!" - Psalm 133:1 (KJV)

The cadence of unity harmonizes the hearts and minds of believers. Just as soldiers march in step to the beat of the drum, so too must you strive for unity in the body of Christ. Reflect on the beauty of unity described in Psalm 133, where brothers and sisters dwell together in harmony. Let this unity be a witness to the world of God's love and power.

Seek to preserve the unity of the Spirit in the bond of peace, bearing with one another in love. For where there is unity, there is strength, and God commands His blessing upon it.

Prayer: Gracious Father, unite us as one body, that we may bear witness to Your love and truth in the world. Help us to walk in humility and love, preserving the unity of the Spirit. Amen.

DAY 28
THE FORTITUDE OF FAITHFULNESS

Scripture: "Moreover it is required in stewards, that a man be found faithful." - 1 Corinthians 4:2 (KJV)

The fortitude of faithfulness sustains you through trials and tribulations. Just as soldiers stand firm in the face of adversity, so too must you remain faithful to the calling and purpose God has placed on your life. Consider the faithfulness of God throughout history, as He remained steadfast in His love and promises to His people. Let His faithfulness inspire you to persevere and endure to the end.

Commit yourself to being a faithful steward of the gifts and opportunities God has entrusted to you. For in faithfulness, you honor Him and bring glory to His name.

Prayer: Faithful God, grant me the strength and courage to remain steadfast in my devotion to You. Help me to be faithful in all things, that I may bring glory to Your name. Amen.

DAY 29
THE COMPASS OF DIVINE DIRECTION

Scripture: "Thy word is a lamp unto my feet, and a light unto my path." - Psalm 119:105 (KJV)

The compass of divine direction guides your steps along the path of righteousness. Just as a compass points true north, so too does God's Word illuminate the way forward in your life. Reflect on the guidance and wisdom found in Scripture, as God reveals His will and purpose for your life. Let His Word be a lamp to your feet, guiding your every decision and action.

Seek divine direction through prayer and meditation, allowing the Holy Spirit to lead and guide you into all truth. For He promises to direct your steps and make your paths straight.

Prayer: Heavenly Father, guide me by Your Spirit and illuminate Your Word as I seek Your direction for my life. Help me to walk in obedience to Your will, trusting in Your guidance and provision. Amen.

DAY 30
THE DRILL OF DILIGENCE

Scripture: "Seest thou a man diligent in his business? he shall stand before kings; he shall not stand before mean men." - Proverbs 22:29 (KJV)

The drill of diligence hones your skills and prepares you for the battles ahead. Just as soldiers undergo rigorous training to excel in warfare, so too must you cultivate diligence and perseverance in every aspect of your life. Consider the example of the ant described in

Proverbs, which works diligently to gather food in the summer. Let this diligence be a hallmark of your character, as you pursue excellence in all that you do.

Commit yourself to the discipline of hard work and dedication, knowing that your efforts will be rewarded. For God honors those who are diligent in their labor, and He will exalt you in due time.

Prayer: Lord, grant me the spirit of diligence and perseverance, that I may excel in every task set before me. Help me to work heartily unto You, knowing that You reward those who diligently seek You. Amen.

DAY 31
THE ORDER OF OBEDIENCE

Scripture: "And Samuel said, Hath the Lord as great delight in burnt offerings and sacrifices, as in obeying the voice of the Lord? Behold, to obey is better than sacrifice, and to hearken than the fat of rams." - 1 Samuel 15:22 (KJV)

The order of obedience is paramount in the life of a believer. Just as soldiers follow orders without question, so too must you obey the commands of the Lord with unwavering faithfulness. Reflect on the story of King Saul, who disobeyed God's command and suffered the consequences. Let his example serve as a warning against the dangers of disobedience and rebellion.

Commit yourself to obeying God's Word wholeheartedly, knowing that His commands are for your good and His glory. For blessed are those who obey His commands, for they will walk in His favor and blessings.

Prayer: Heavenly Father, grant me the grace to obey Your Word without hesitation or reservation. Help me to walk in obedience to Your commands, trusting in Your wisdom and sovereignty. Amen.

DAY 32
THE RESILIENCE OF THE RIGHTEOUS

Scripture: "The righteous shall flourish like the palm tree: he shall grow like a cedar in Lebanon." - Psalm 92:12 (KJV)

The resilience of the righteous is a testament to the strength of their faith. Just as trees withstand storms and adversity, so too do the righteous endure trials and tribulations with unwavering faith. Consider the imagery of the palm tree and cedar in Psalm 92, which symbolize the steadfastness and endurance of the righteous. Let their example inspire you to stand firm in your faith, rooted and grounded in the love of Christ.

Prayer: Gracious God, strengthen me with Your power to endure trials and tribulations with unwavering faith. Help me to stand firm in Your promises, knowing that You are my refuge and strength. Amen.

DAY 33
THE WARFARE OF WORSHIP

Scripture: "Yet thou art holy, O thou that inhabitest the praises of Israel." - Psalm 22:3 (KJV)

The warfare of worship is a powerful weapon against the forces of darkness. Just as soldiers wield their weapons in battle, so too do believers engage in spiritual warfare through the weapon of worship. Reflect on the story of King Jehoshaphat, who defeated his enemies through the power of worship and praise. Let his example inspire you to lift up your voice in praise and adoration to the Lord.

Prayer: Mighty God, teach me to wield the weapon of worship effectively in spiritual warfare. Help me to praise You with all my heart, knowing that You inhabit the praises of Your people. Amen.

DAY 34
THE ALLY OF ALTRUISM

Scripture: "Bear ye one another's burdens, and so fulfil the law of Christ." - Galatians 6:2 (KJV)

Altruism, the selfless concern for the well-being of others, is a powerful ally in the kingdom of God. Just as soldiers watch each other's backs in battle, so too must believers support and encourage one another in love. Consider the example of Jesus, who laid down His life for us out of love and compassion. Let His sacrificial love inspire you to selflessly serve others, bearing their burdens and sharing in their joys.

Prayer: Loving Father, fill me with Your love and compassion for others, that I may selflessly serve and support them. Help me to bear one another's burdens and fulfil the law of Christ. Amen.

DAY 35
THE BARRACKS OF BROTHERHOOD

Scripture: "Behold, how good and how pleasant it is for brethren to dwell together in unity!" - Psalm 133:1 (KJV)

The barracks of brotherhood is a place of unity and fellowship among believers. Just as soldiers form strong bonds of camaraderie in the barracks, so too must believers cultivate unity and love among one another. Reflect on the beauty of unity described in Psalm 133, where brothers and sisters dwell together in harmony. Let this unity be a witness to the world of God's love and power.

Prayer: Gracious Father, unite us as one body, that we may bear witness to Your love and truth in the world. Help us to walk in humility and love, preserving the unity of the Spirit. Amen.

DAY 36
THE VIGILANCE OF VIRTUE

Scripture: "Finally, brethren, whatsoever things are true, whatsoever things are honest, whatsoever things are just, whatsoever things are pure, whatsoever things are lovely, whatsoever things are of good report; if there be any virtue, and if there be any praise, think on these things." - Philippians 4:8 (KJV)

The vigilance of virtue requires constant attention to that which is good and noble. Just as a soldier remains vigilant on guard duty, so too must you guard your heart and mind against the influences of the world. Reflect on the virtues outlined in Philippians 4:8, which serve as a guide for righteous living. Let your thoughts be consumed with that which is true, honest, just, and pure, dwelling on the things that are praiseworthy and of good report.

Prayer: Heavenly Father, help me to cultivate virtue in my life, guarding my heart and mind against the influences of the world. May my thoughts be pleasing to You, and may I reflect Your goodness and righteousness in all that I do. Amen.

DAY 37
THE OPERATIONS OF OPTIMISM

Scripture: "And we know that all things work together for good to them that love God, to them who are the called according to his purpose." - Romans 8:28 (KJV)

The operations of optimism are grounded in the assurance that God works all things together for good. Just as a skilled strategist sees opportunity in the midst of adversity, so too must you maintain a positive outlook in every situation. Reflect on the promise of Romans 8:28, which assures believers that God's providence is at work in their lives. Let this truth fill you with hope and confidence, knowing that He who began a good work in you will bring it to completion.

Prayer: Lord, grant me the gift of optimism, that I may see Your hand at work in every circumstance. Help me to trust in Your providence and to maintain a positive outlook, knowing that You are working all things together for my good. Amen.

DAY 38
THE TACTICS OF TRUST

Scripture: "Trust in the Lord with all thine heart; and lean not unto thine own understanding. In all thy ways acknowledge him, and he shall direct thy paths." - Proverbs 3:5-6 (KJV)

The tactics of trust require surrendering your will to God's perfect plan. Just as a soldier trust in the orders of his commanding officer, so too must you trust in the wisdom and guidance of the Lord. Reflect on the wisdom of Proverbs 3:5-6, which exhorts believers to trust in the Lord with all their hearts and lean not on their own understanding. Let your trust in God be unwavering, acknowledging His sovereignty in every aspect of your life.

Prayer: Gracious Father, teach me to trust in You with all my heart, leaning not on my own understanding. Guide me in Your paths of righteousness, and help me to surrender my will to Your perfect plan. Amen.

DAY 39
THE RECON OF RESILIENCE

Scripture: "And not only so, but we glory in tribulations also: knowing that tribulation worketh patience; And patience, experience; and experience, hope." - Romans 5:3-4 (KJV)

The recon of resilience involves facing trials with courage and perseverance. Just as a soldier gathers intelligence before engaging the enemy, so too must you gather strength and wisdom through trials. Reflect on the words of Romans 5:3-4, which speak of the transformative power of tribulation. Let your trials be opportunities for growth, knowing that they produce patience, experience, and hope.

Prayer: Lord, grant me the resilience to endure trials with courage and perseverance. May my tribulations be opportunities for growth and transformation, as You work in me to produce patience, experience, and hope. Amen.

DAY 40
THE DEPLOYMENT OF DEVOTION

Scripture: "And thou shalt love the Lord thy God with all thy heart, and with all thy soul, and with all thy mind, and with all thy strength: this is the first commandment." - Mark 12:30 (KJV)

The deployment of devotion involves wholehearted love and commitment to God. Just as a soldier is fully committed to the mission, so too must you devote yourself entirely to loving and serving the Lord. Reflect on the commandment in Mark 12:30, which calls believers to love the Lord with all their heart, soul, mind, and strength. Let your devotion to God be evident in every aspect of your life, as you seek to glorify Him in all that you do.

Prayer: Heavenly Father, help me to deploy my devotion to You wholeheartedly, loving You with all my being. May my life be a reflection of Your love and grace, as I seek to honor You in every area of my life. Amen.

DAY 41
THE STRATEGY OF SELF-CONTROL

Scripture: "For God hath not given us the spirit of fear; but of power, and of love, and of a sound mind." - 2 Timothy 1:7 (KJV)

The strategy of self-control is essential in the life of a believer. Just as a skilled general exercises discipline and restraint in battle, so too must you exercise self-control in every area of your life. Reflect on the wisdom of 2 Timothy 1:7, which reminds us that God has given us a spirit of power, love, and a sound mind. Let His Spirit empower you to exercise self-control over your thoughts, words, and actions.

Prayer: Heavenly Father, grant me the strength and wisdom to exercise self-control in every area of my life. Help me to yield to Your Spirit and walk in the power of Your love, exercising discipline and restraint. Amen.

DAY 42
THE LOGISTICS OF LOVE

Scripture: "And above all things have fervent charity among yourselves: for charity shall cover the multitude of sins." - 1 Peter 4:8 (KJV)

The logistics of love involve the practical application of love in everyday life. Just as a skilled logistician coordinate supplies and resources for the army, so too must you coordinate acts of love and kindness toward others. Reflect on the command in 1 Peter 4:8 to have fervent charity among yourselves. Let love be the driving force behind all your actions, covering a multitude of sins and bringing healing and restoration.

Prayer: Gracious Father, teach me to love others fervently, as You have loved me. May my acts of love and kindness bring glory to Your name and reflect Your heart of compassion and grace. Amen.

DAY 43
THE GARRISON OF GRATITUDE

Scripture: "In everything give thanks: for this is the will of God in Christ Jesus concerning you." - 1 Thessalonians 5:18 (KJV)

The garrison of gratitude is a stronghold against discouragement and despair. Just as a garrison fortifies a city against attack, so too does gratitude fortify your heart against the assaults of the enemy. Reflect on the command in 1 Thessalonians 5:18 to give thanks in everything. Let gratitude be your constant companion, even in the midst of trials and tribulations, knowing that God is faithful and His promises are true.

Prayer: Heavenly Father, help me to cultivate a heart of gratitude in all circumstances. May thankfulness be my constant companion, as I trust in Your faithfulness and goodness. Amen.

DAY 44
THE SENTINEL'S SOLITUDE

Scripture: "But thou, when thou prays, enter into thy closet, and when thou hast shut thy door, pray to thy Father which is in secret; and thy Father which seeth in secret shall reward thee openly." - Matthew 6:6 (KJV)

The sentinel's solitude is a sacred time of communion with God. Just as a sentinel stands watch alone, so too must you carve out moments of solitude to seek the presence and guidance of the Lord. Reflect on the instruction of Jesus in Matthew 6:6 to pray in secret. Let your time alone with God be a sanctuary for your soul, where you can pour out your heart in prayer and listen for His still, small voice.

Prayer: Lord, in the solitude of this moment, I come to seek Your face and hear Your voice. Speak to me, O God, and guide me in Your ways. May this time of communion with You strengthen my spirit and renew my resolve to follow You. Amen.

DAY 45
THE CADET'S CALL TO COURAGE

Scripture: "Be strong and of a good courage, fear not, nor be afraid of them: for the Lord thy God, he it is that doth go with thee; he will not fail thee, nor forsake thee." - Deuteronomy 31:6 (KJV)

The cadet's call to courage echoes the command of God to His people. Just as cadets are trained to be courageous in the face of danger, so too must you be strong and courageous, knowing that the Lord your God goes with you. Reflect on the promise in Deuteronomy 31:6 that God will never leave you nor forsake you. Let this assurance embolden you to face every challenge and obstacle with courage and faith.

Prayer: Heavenly Father, grant me the courage to face every trial and challenge with confidence, knowing that You are with me. Strengthen my faith and embolden my spirit, that I may walk in courage and obedience to Your will. Amen.

DAY 46
THE OFFICER'S OATH OF OFFICE

Scripture: "And thou shalt teach them diligently unto thy children, and shalt talk of them when thou sittest in thine house, and when thou walkest by the way, and when thou liest down, and when thou risest up." - Deuteronomy 6:7 (KJV)

The officer's oath of office is a solemn commitment to uphold truth and justice. Just as officers pledge to defend their nation, so too must you pledge to uphold the teachings of God's Word in every aspect of your life. Reflect on the command in Deuteronomy 6:7 to teach God's Word diligently to your children. Let your life be a living testimony to the principles of truth and righteousness, as you walk in obedience to His commands.

Prayer: Gracious Father, help me to uphold Your truth and justice in every aspect of my life. Grant me the wisdom and courage to fulfill my oath of office, teaching Your Word diligently to those around me. Amen.

DAY 47
THE DRILL SERGEANT'S DISCIPLINE

Scripture: "For whom the Lord loveth he chasteneth, and scourgeth every son whom he receiveth." - Hebrews 12:6 (KJV)

The drill sergeant's discipline molds soldiers into warriors. Just as a drill sergeant pushes recruits to their limits, so too does God discipline His children out of love to shape them into vessels of honor. Reflect on the truth of Hebrews 12:6, which reminds us that God disciplines those He loves. Let His discipline refine your character and strengthen your resolve to walk in obedience and righteousness.

Prayer: Heavenly Father, thank You for Your loving discipline in my life. Help me to embrace correction with humility and gratitude, knowing that You are shaping me into the person You created me to be. Amen.

DAY 48
THE WARRIOR'S WISDOM

Scripture: "The fear of the Lord is the beginning of wisdom: and the knowledge of the holy is understanding." - Proverbs 9:10 (KJV)

The warrior's wisdom begins with the fear of the Lord. Just as a wise general considers the consequences of every decision, so too must you seek wisdom from God's Word to navigate the challenges of life. Reflect on the wisdom of Proverbs 9:10, which teaches that true wisdom begins with reverence for God. Let your decisions be guided by His Word and His Spirit, trusting in His guidance and direction.

Prayer: Wise God, grant me discernment and understanding as I seek Your wisdom in all things. Help me to fear You and walk in obedience to Your Word, trusting in Your guidance and direction. Amen.

DAY 49
THE CHAPLAIN'S COMPASSION

Scripture: "Let nothing be done through strife or vainglory; but in lowliness of mind let each esteem other better than themselves." - Philippians 2:3 (KJV)

The chaplain's compassion flows from a heart of humility and love. Just as a chaplain minister to the needs of soldiers with compassion, so too must you show kindness and empathy to those around you.

Reflect on the exhortation in Philippians 2:3 to esteem others better than yourselves. Let compassion be the hallmark of your character, as you follow the example of Jesus in serving others with humility and grace.

Prayer: Compassionate Father, fill me with Your love and empathy for those around me. Help me to minister to others with humility and grace, showing kindness and compassion as You have shown to me. Amen.

DAY 50
THE SENTRY'S STEADFASTNESS

Scripture: "Watch ye, stand fast in the faith, quit you like men, be strong." - 1 Corinthians 16:13 (KJV)

The sentry's steadfastness is a beacon of strength in times of trial. Just as a sentry stands guard with unwavering vigilance, so too must you stand firm in your faith, resolute in the face of adversity. Reflect on the exhortation in 1 Corinthians 16:13 to stand fast in the faith. Let your faith be an anchor for your soul, grounding you in the promises of God and giving you strength to endure every trial.

Prayer: Almighty God, grant me the strength and courage to stand firm in my faith, even in the midst of trials and tribulations. Help me to be a beacon of hope and steadfastness to those around me. Amen.

DAY 51
THE ARTILLERY OF ADORATION

Scripture: "But thou art holy, O thou that inhabitest the praises of Israel." - Psalm 22:3 (KJV)

The artillery of adoration is a powerful weapon in spiritual warfare. Just as artillery strikes the enemy's stronghold, so too does our worship and adoration of God break through the strongholds of darkness. Reflect on the truth of Psalm 22:3, which declares that God inhabits the praises of His people. When we lift our voices in adoration and worship, His presence fills our midst, dispelling fear and doubt.

Prayer: Gracious God, I come before You with adoration and praise. May my worship be a powerful weapon in spiritual warfare, breaking through every stronghold of darkness. Fill me with Your presence as I lift my voice in adoration and praise. Amen.

DAY 52
THE COMBATANT'S COMPASS

Scripture: "Thy word is a lamp unto my feet, and a light unto my path." - Psalm 119:105 (KJV)

The combatant's compass is the Word of God. Just as a compass guides a traveler through unknown terrain, so too does God's Word guide us through the trials and challenges of life. Reflect on the truth of Psalm 119:105, which compares God's Word to a lamp that illuminates our path. In times of confusion and uncertainty, His Word provides clarity and direction.

Prayer: Heavenly Father, thank You for Your Word, which is a lamp unto my feet and a light unto my path. Help me to navigate the challenges of life with wisdom and discernment, guided by Your Word. Amen.

DAY 53
THE STRATEGY OF SERENITY

Scripture: "Be careful for nothing; but in everything by prayer and supplication with thanksgiving let your requests be made known unto God. And the peace of God, which passeth all understanding, shall keep your hearts and minds through Christ Jesus." - Philippians 4:6-7 (KJV)

The strategy of serenity involves trusting God with all your cares and worries. Just as a skilled general remains calm under pressure, so too must you find peace in the midst of life's storms by placing your trust in God. Reflect on the promise in Philippians 4:6-7, which assures us that the peace of God, which surpasses all understanding, will guard our hearts and minds in Christ Jesus.

Prayer: Lord, grant me the serenity to trust You with all my cares and worries. May Your peace, which surpasses all understanding, guard my heart and mind in Christ Jesus. Amen.

DAY 54

THE WARRIOR'S WATCHFULNESS

Scripture: "Watch ye, stand fast in the faith, quit you like men, be strong." - 1 Corinthians 16:13 (KJV)

The warrior's watchfulness involves being vigilant and alert to the schemes of the enemy. Just as a sentinel stands watch over the city, so too must you be vigilant in guarding your heart and mind against the attacks of the enemy. Reflect on the exhortation in 1 Corinthians 16:13 to be watchful and stand firm in the faith. In a world filled with spiritual warfare, we must remain vigilant and alert, standing firm in our faith.

Prayer: Almighty God, help me to be vigilant and alert to the schemes of the enemy. Grant me the strength to stand firm in the faith, being watchful and sober-minded. Amen.

DAY 55

THE BATTLEFIELD OF BELIEF

Scripture: "Jesus said unto him, If thou canst believe, all things are possible to him that believeth." - Mark 9:23 (KJV)

The battlefield of belief is where faith is tested and victories are won. Just as a soldier must believe in the cause for which he fights, so too must you believe in the promises of God and His power to overcome every obstacle. Reflect on the words of Jesus in Mark 9:23, which declare that all things are possible to him who believes. In the face of doubt and adversity, let your faith be unwavering, knowing that God is faithful to fulfill His promises.

Prayer: Faithful Father, strengthen my belief in Your promises and Your power. Help me to stand firm in faith, knowing that all things are possible to him who believes. Amen.

DAY 56
THE DISCIPLINE OF DEDICATION

Scripture: "I beseech you therefore, brethren, by the mercies of God, that ye present your bodies a living sacrifice, holy, acceptable unto God, which is your reasonable service." - Romans 12:1 (KJV)

The discipline of dedication calls for a life wholly surrendered to God. Just as a soldier dedicates themselves to their duty, so too must you offer your entire being as a living sacrifice to God, holy and pleasing to Him. Reflect on the exhortation in Romans 12:1, which urges believers to present themselves as living sacrifices. Let your dedication to God be evident in every aspect of your life, as you seek to honor Him with your thoughts, words, and actions.

Prayer: Heavenly Father, I dedicate myself afresh to You today. May my life be a living sacrifice, holy and pleasing to You. Help me to walk in obedience and dedication, honoring You in all that I do. Amen.

DAY 57
THE SENTINEL'S SERENITY

Scripture: "I will both lay me down in peace, and sleep: for thou, Lord, only makest me dwell in safety." - Psalm 4:8 (KJV)

The sentinel's serenity comes from trusting in God's protection. Just as a sentinel rests in the assurance of safety, so too can you find peace and serenity in the knowledge that God watches over you. Reflect on the promise in Psalm 4:8, which declares that God alone makes us dwell in safety. Let His presence surround you with peace and comfort, even in the midst of uncertainty and danger.

Prayer: Gracious God, thank You for Your constant protection and care. Grant me the serenity to rest in Your peace, knowing that You watch over me and keep me safe. Amen.

DAY 58
THE WARRIOR'S WILL

Scripture: "And let us not be weary in well doing: for in due season we shall reap, if we faint not." - Galatians 6:9 (KJV)

The warrior's will perseveres in the face of adversity. Just as a warrior presses on despite fatigue and hardship, so too must you remain steadfast in doing good, knowing that a reward awaits those who endure. Reflect on the encouragement in Galatians 6:9, which reminds us not to grow weary in doing good. Let your will be strengthened by faith, trusting in God's promise of a harvest of blessings for those who persevere.

Prayer: Lord, strengthen my will to persevere in doing good, even when I face trials and difficulties. Help me to trust in Your promise of a harvest of blessings, knowing that You are faithful to fulfill Your word. Amen.

DAY 59
THE COMMANDER'S COMPASSION

Scripture: "And be ye kind one to another, tender-hearted, forgiving one another, even as God for Christ's sake hath forgiven you." - Ephesians 4:32 (KJV)

The commander's compassion reflects God's mercy and grace. Just as a commander shows compassion to their troops, so too must you extend kindness and forgiveness to others, as God has forgiven you. Reflect on the command in Ephesians 4:32 to be kind and compassionate, forgiving one another as God has forgiven you. Let His compassion flow through you, touching the lives of those around you with grace and mercy.

Prayer: Loving Father, help me to show compassion and kindness to others, just as You have shown to me. Grant me a tender heart and a forgiving spirit, reflecting Your love and mercy to those around me. Amen.

DAY 60
THE TROOPER'S TRUST

Scripture: "For the Lord shall be thy confidence, and shall keep thy foot from being taken." - Proverbs 3:26 (KJV)

The trooper's trust is anchored in God's faithfulness. Just as a trooper trust in their training and equipment, so too must you trust in the Lord to guide and protect you from stumbling. Reflect on the promise in Proverbs 3:26, which assures us that the Lord will be our confidence and keep us from falling. Let your trust in God's faithfulness give you confidence and peace, knowing that He is with you every step of the way.

Prayer: Faithful God, I trust in Your unfailing love and protection. May Your presence be my confidence, and Your guidance keep me from stumbling. Help me to trust in You with all my heart and lean not on my own understanding. Amen.

DAY 61
THE DRILL OF DISCIPLINE

Scripture: "For whom the Lord loveth he chasteneth, and scourgeth every son whom he receiveth." - Hebrews 12:6 (KJV)

The drill of discipline molds character and shapes destiny. Just as a soldier endures rigorous training, so too must you embrace the discipline of God, knowing that it refines and strengthens you for His purposes. Reflect on Hebrews 12:6, which reminds us that God disciplines those He loves. His correction is not punishment but a loving guidance towards growth and maturity.

Prayer: Heavenly Father, help me embrace the discipline that leads to godliness. Grant me the humility to submit to Your correction and the strength to endure the refining process. May Your discipline mold me into the person You desire me to be. Amen.

DAY 62
THE MARCH OF MINDFULNESS

Scripture: "Finally, brethren, whatsoever things are true, whatsoever things are honest, whatsoever things are just, whatsoever things are pure, whatsoever things are lovely, whatsoever things are of good report; if there be any virtue, and if there be any praise, think on these things." - Philippians 4:8 (KJV)

The march of mindfulness is a deliberate focus on God's truth and goodness. Just as a soldier maintains awareness of their surroundings, so too must you cultivate mindfulness in your thoughts and actions. Reflect on Philippians 4:8, which instructs us to dwell on things that are true, noble, right, pure, lovely, and admirable. By fixing your thoughts on God's goodness, you'll find peace and clarity in every step.

Prayer: Gracious God, help me to be mindful of Your presence in every moment. Guide my thoughts and actions to reflect Your truth and goodness. May my life be a testament to Your grace and love. Amen.

DAY 63
THE CADENCE OF KINDNESS

Scripture: "But love ye your enemies, and do good, and lend, hoping for nothing again; and your reward shall be great, and ye shall be the children of the Highest: for he is kind unto the unthankful and to the evil." - Luke 6:35 (KJV)

The cadence of kindness sets the rhythm of your life. Just as a soldier marches in step, so too must you walk in the cadence of God's love, showing kindness and mercy to all.

Reflect on Luke 6:35, which challenges us to love our enemies and do good to those who mistreat us. By extending kindness, you reflect the character of our Heavenly Father.

Prayer: Loving Father, teach me to walk in the cadence of Your kindness. Help me to love others as You have loved me, showing mercy and compassion to all. May Your kindness shine through me, drawing others to Your love. Amen.

DAY 64
THE WARRIOR'S WATCH

Scripture: "Watch ye, stand fast in the faith, quit you like men, be strong." - 1 Corinthians 16:13 (KJV)

The warrior's watch requires vigilance and readiness. Just as a sentinel stands guard, so too must you be alert and vigilant, guarding your heart and mind against the schemes of the enemy.

Reflect on 1 Corinthians 16:13, which calls us to be watchful and steadfast in our faith. By staying vigilant and alert, you'll be prepared to resist temptation and stand firm in the face of adversity.

Prayer: Almighty God, help me to be vigilant and watchful in my walk with You. Grant me strength to resist the attacks of the enemy and courage to stand firm in my faith. May Your Holy Spirit guide and protect me each day. Amen.

DAY 65
THE SOLDIER'S STEADFAST LOVE

Scripture: "Beloved, let us love one another: for love is of God; and every one that loveth is born of God, and knoweth God." - 1 John 4:7 (KJV)

The soldier's steadfast love reflects the love of our Heavenly Father. Just as a soldier remains loyal to their comrades, so too must you demonstrate unwavering love for others, for love is the hallmark of true discipleship.

Reflect on 1 John 4:7, which declares that love is of God. By loving others, you reveal the character of God and bear witness to His transforming grace.

Prayer: Gracious Father, fill me with Your steadfast love that I may love others as You have loved me. Help me to demonstrate Your love in all I do, reflecting Your grace and mercy to a world in need. Amen.

DAY 66
THE OFFICER'S ORDERLINESS

Scripture: "Let all things be done decently and in order." - 1 Corinthians 14:40 (KJV)

The officer's orderliness brings structure and clarity. Just as an officer maintains order and discipline, so too must you bring order to your life, ensuring that all things are done decently and in order.

Reflect on 1 Corinthians 14:40, which emphasizes the importance of orderliness in all things. By maintaining order in your life, you create space for God to work and bring about His plans and purposes.

Prayer: Heavenly Father, help me to bring order to my life according to Your will. Grant me wisdom to prioritize the things that matter most and to cultivate habits of discipline and orderliness. May my life bring glory to Your name. Amen.

DAY 67
THE CADET'S COMMITMENT

Scripture: "Commit thy way unto the Lord; trust also in him; and he shall bring it to pass." - Psalm 37:5 (KJV)

The cadet's commitment is unwavering and steadfast. Just as a cadet commits to their training, so too must you commit your ways to the Lord, trusting in His faithfulness to bring His plans to fruition.

Reflect on Psalm 37:5, which encourages us to commit our ways to the Lord. By entrusting your life to His care, you'll find strength and courage to persevere through every challenge.

Prayer: Faithful God, I commit my life into Your hands today. Grant me the strength and courage to follow You wholeheartedly, trusting in Your faithfulness to fulfill Your promises. May my commitment to You be unwavering and steadfast. Amen.

DAY 68
THE GENERAL'S GRACE

Scripture: "But he giveth more grace. Wherefore he saith, God resisteth the proud, but giveth grace unto the humble." - James 4:6 (KJV)

The general's grace flows from humility and wisdom. Just as a general extends grace to their troops, so too does our Heavenly Father lavish His grace upon the humble and contrite of heart.

Reflect on James 4:6, which reminds us that God gives grace to the humble. By humbling yourself before Him, you open the floodgates of His grace and mercy in your life.

Prayer: Gracious Father, thank You for Your abundant grace and mercy. Help me to walk in humility before You, acknowledging my need for Your grace in every area of my life. May Your grace abound in me, bringing glory to Your name. Amen.

DAY 69
THE DRILL INSTRUCTOR'S DETERMINATION

Scripture: "And let us not be weary in well doing: for in due season we shall reap, if we faint not." - Galatians 6:9 (KJV)

The drill instructor's determination inspires excellence and perseverance. Just as a drill instructor pushes their recruits to their limits, so too does God encourage us to press on in faith, knowing that our labor is not in vain.

Reflect on Galatians 6:9, which urges us not to grow weary in doing good. By remaining determined and steadfast in our commitment to Christ, we'll reap a harvest of blessings in due time.

Prayer: Almighty God, grant me the determination to persevere in faith and obedience. Strengthen me to press on in doing good, knowing that You will reward those who remain faithful to the end. May Your Spirit empower me to run the race with endurance. Amen.

DAY 70
THE CHAPLAIN'S CHARITY

Scripture: "And now abideth faith, hope, charity, these three; but the greatest of these is charity." - 1 Corinthians 13:13 (KJV)

The chaplain's charity exemplifies God's love in action. Just as a chaplain minister to the needs of others with compassion, so too must you extend charity and kindness to those around you, for love is the greatest of all virtues.

Reflect on 1 Corinthians 13:13, which declares that the greatest of all virtues is charity, or love. By showing love and compassion to others, you reflect the heart of our Heavenly Father.

Prayer: Loving Father, fill me with Your love that I may show charity and kindness to those around me. Help me to be a vessel of Your love, ministering to the needs of others with compassion and grace. May Your love shine brightly through me, drawing others into Your embrace. Amen.

DAY 71
THE RESILIENCE OF THE RIGHTEOUS - DRAWING STRENGTH FROM THE STORIES OF VALOR

Scripture: "The righteous cry, and the Lord heareth, and delivereth them out of all their troubles." - Psalm 34:17 (KJV)

The resilience of the righteous is rooted in unwavering faith and trust in God. Just as the righteous of old cried out to the Lord in their trials, so too can you draw strength from their stories of valor and triumph. Reflect on Psalm 34:17, which assures us that the Lord hears the cries of the righteous and delivers them from all their troubles. Let the stories of biblical heroes and saints inspire you to persevere in faith, knowing that God is faithful to uphold His children.

Prayer: Heavenly Father, thank You for the examples of resilience and faith found in Your Word. As I face challenges, help me to draw strength from the stories of Your faithful servants. Grant me the resilience to persevere, knowing that You are with me always. Amen.

DAY 72

THE COURAGE TO CONQUER - LEARNING FROM THE VICTORIES OF PAST MILITARY LEADERS

Scripture: "Be strong and of a good courage, fear not, nor be afraid of them: for the Lord thy God, he it is that doth go with thee; he will not fail thee, nor forsake thee." - Deuteronomy 31:6 (KJV)

The courage to conquer is forged in the crucible of adversity and inspired by the triumphs of past military leaders. Just as Joshua led the Israelites into the Promised Land with courage and faith, so too can you learn from the victories of those who have gone before you. Reflect on Deuteronomy 31:6, which reassures us that God goes with us and will never fail or forsake us. Let the stories of courageous leaders throughout history embolden you to face your challenges with faith and determination.

Prayer: Almighty God, thank You for the examples of courage and leadership in history. As I strive to overcome obstacles, may I draw inspiration from the courage of past military leaders. Grant me the strength and courage to conquer, knowing that You are with me every step of the way. Amen.

DAY 73

THE STRATEGY OF STILLNESS - EMBRACING CALM AMIDST CHAOS

Scripture: "Be still, and know that I am God: I will be exalted among the heathen, I will be exalted in the earth." - Psalm 46:10 (KJV)

The strategy of stillness is a powerful weapon in the midst of chaos and turmoil. Just as a soldier finds calm amidst the storm, so too can you find peace and clarity by resting in God's presence. Reflect on Psalm 46:10, which calls us to be still and know that God is in control. In moments of chaos and uncertainty, take refuge in His presence and trust in His sovereignty over all things.

Prayer: Gracious Father, in the midst of chaos and turmoil, help me to find stillness in Your presence. Grant me the peace that surpasses all understanding as I rest in Your sovereignty. May Your peace reign in my heart and mind, even in the midst of the storm. Amen.

DAY 74

THE DISCIPLINE OF THE DEDICATED - THE POWER OF UNWAVERING COMMITMENT

Scripture: "And whatsoever ye do, do it heartily, as to the Lord, and not unto men." - Colossians 3:23 (KJV)

The discipline of the dedicated is marked by unwavering commitment and wholehearted devotion. Just as a soldier is disciplined in their training and duties, so too must you commit yourself wholeheartedly to the tasks set before you. Reflect on Colossians 3:23, which urges us to do everything as unto the Lord. Whether in times of ease or hardship, let your dedication be unwavering, knowing that your labor is not in vain in the Lord.

Prayer: Heavenly Father, help me to cultivate unwavering commitment and dedication in all that I do. May my efforts be pleasing unto You, knowing that You are the ultimate rewarder of those who diligently seek You. Strengthen me to persevere in faithfulness and devotion. Amen.

DAY 75
THE WISDOM OF THE WARRIOR - GLEANING INSIGHTS FROM HISTORICAL BATTLES

Scripture: "For by wise counsel thou shalt make thy war: and in multitude of counsellors there is safety." - Proverbs 24:6 (KJV)

The wisdom of the warrior is found in learning from the lessons of history and seeking wise counsel. Just as military leaders study past battles to gain insights for future victories, so too can you glean wisdom from the experiences of others. Reflect on Proverbs 24:6, which emphasizes the importance of wise counsel in making decisions. Seek guidance from those who have walked the path before you, and learn from their experiences to navigate the challenges you face.

Prayer: Gracious Father, grant me wisdom and discernment as I seek to learn from the lessons of history. Help me to surround myself with wise counselors who can offer guidance and insight. May I walk in the wisdom of the warrior, making sound decisions that honor You. Amen.

DAY 76

THE HONOR OF HUMILITY - THE QUIET STRENGTH OF THE HUMBLE HERO

Scripture: "He hath shewed thee, O man, what is good; and what doth the Lord require of thee, but to do justly, and to love mercy, and to walk humbly with thy God?" - Micah 6:8 (KJV)

The honor of humility is the mark of a true hero. Just as Jesus humbled Himself to serve others, so too must you embrace humility as a virtue of true greatness. Reflect on Micah 6:8, which reveals God's requirements for us: to do justly, love mercy, and walk humbly with Him. Let humility be the foundation of your character, knowing that God exalts the humble and lifts them up in due time.

Prayer: Loving Father, help me to walk humbly before You and others, following the example of Your Son, Jesus Christ. Grant me the strength to serve with humility and grace, reflecting Your love and mercy to a world in need. May my life bring honor and glory to Your name. Amen.

DAY 77

THE LEGACY OF LEADERSHIP - WHAT HISTORY TEACHES US ABOUT LEADING WITH INTEGRITY

Scripture: "But as for you, be strong and do not give up, for your work will be rewarded." - 2 Chronicles 15:7 (NIV)

The legacy of leadership is built on a foundation of integrity and perseverance. Just as leaders of old faced trials and challenges with courage and determination, so too can you leave a lasting legacy by leading with integrity and honor. Reflect on 2 Chronicles 15:7, which encourages us to be strong and not give up, for our work will be rewarded. Let the examples of leaders from history inspire you to lead with courage and conviction, knowing that God rewards faithfulness.

Prayer: Almighty God, thank You for the examples of leadership found throughout history. Grant me the strength and wisdom to lead with integrity and honor, following in the footsteps of those who have gone before me. May my leadership leave a legacy that honors You. Amen.

DAY 78

THE VALOR OF VIRTUE - REFLECTING ON MORAL COURAGE IN THE LINE OF DUTY

Scripture: "Watch ye, stand fast in the faith, quit you like men, be strong." - 1 Corinthians 16:13 (KJV)

The valor of virtue is seen in the moral courage to stand firm in the face of adversity. Just as soldiers stand fast in battle, so too must you uphold the virtues of righteousness and integrity, even in the most challenging circumstances.

Reflect on 1 Corinthians 16:13, which calls us to be strong and stand firm in the faith. Let your life be a testament to the courage that comes from walking in obedience to God's Word, even when it requires sacrifice.

Prayer: Gracious Father, grant me the courage to uphold virtue and righteousness in all areas of my life. Strengthen me to stand firm in the face of adversity, trusting in Your power and presence to sustain me. May my life bring honor to Your name. Amen.

DAY 79

THE FAITHFUL LEADER - LESSONS FROM
HISTORIC MILITARY CHAPLAINS

Scripture: "Be thou faithful unto death, and I will give thee a crown of life." - Revelation 2:10 (KJV)

The faithful leader follows the example of historic military chaplains, who ministered to the spiritual needs of soldiers with unwavering devotion. Just as they remained faithful unto death, so too can you strive to be faithful in your leadership, knowing that God rewards faithfulness with the crown of life. Reflect on Revelation 2:10, which promises a crown of life to those who remain faithful unto death. Let the examples of faithful leaders inspire you to lead with dedication and commitment, knowing that your labor in the Lord is not in vain.

Prayer: Heavenly Father, grant me the grace to be a faithful leader, serving with dedication and commitment. Help me to minister to the spiritual needs of others with compassion and grace, following the example of historic military chaplains. May my life bring glory to Your name. Amen.

DAY 80

THE QUIET WARRIOR - THE POWER OF SILENT STRENGTH.

Scripture: "But they that wait upon the Lord shall renew their strength; they shall mount up with wings as eagles; they shall run, and not be weary; and they shall walk, and not faint." - Isaiah 40:31 (KJV)

The quiet warrior draws strength from God's presence, finding renewal and endurance in times of trial. Just as a soldier waits upon the Lord for strength and guidance, so too can you find power in silent strength, trusting in God's provision and care. Reflect on Isaiah 40:31, which assures us that those who wait upon the Lord will renew their strength. Let the quiet moments of waiting on God fill you with His peace and strength, enabling you to face every challenge with confidence.

Prayer: Gracious Father, teach me the power of silent strength as I wait upon You. Renew my strength and endurance, that I may face every trial with confidence and trust in Your provision. May Your presence sustain me in all things. Amen.

DAY 81

THE BATTLE WITHIN - OVERCOMING PERSONAL STRUGGLES

Scripture: "For the flesh lusteth against the Spirit, and the Spirit against the flesh: and these are contrary the one to the other: so that ye cannot do the things that ye would." - Galatians 5:17 (KJV)

The battle within rages as our fleshly desires clash with the desires of the Spirit. Just as soldiers face adversaries on the battlefield, so too must you confront your personal struggles with courage and resolve. Reflect on Galatians 5:17, which vividly depicts the internal conflict between the flesh and the Spirit. In moments of temptation and struggle, rely on the strength of the Spirit to overcome, knowing that God's power is made perfect in weakness.

Prayer: Heavenly Father, grant me the strength to overcome the battles within. Help me to walk in the Spirit, resisting the desires of the flesh. Fill me with Your power and grace, that I may conquer every struggle and live in victory. Amen.

DAY 82

THE HEART OF A HERO - EXPLORING THE CORE VALUES THAT DEFINE TRUE HEROISM

Scripture: "Greater love hath no man than this, that a man lay down his life for his friends." - John 15:13 (KJV)

The heart of a hero beats with sacrificial love and unwavering courage. Just as Jesus laid down His life for us, true heroism is defined by selflessness and love for others. Reflect on John 15:13, which reveals the ultimate expression of love through sacrificial action. Let the core values of love, courage, and selflessness inspire you to live a life of true heroism, serving others with humility and compassion.

Prayer: Gracious Father, thank You for the example of true heroism found in Your Son, Jesus Christ. Help me to embody the core values of love, courage, and selflessness in all that I do. May my life be a reflection of Your love to those around me. Amen.

DAY 83
THE PRAYERFUL PROTECTOR - THE ROLE OF PRAYER IN SAFEGUARDING THE SPIRIT

Scripture: "Pray without ceasing." - 1 Thessalonians 5:17 (KJV)

The prayerful protector finds strength and guidance through constant communion with God. Just as soldiers rely on their weapons for protection, so too must you arm yourself with prayer to safeguard your spirit from spiritual attacks. Reflect on 1 Thessalonians 5:17, which exhorts us to pray without ceasing. Let prayer be your shield and fortress, guarding your heart and mind against the schemes of the enemy.

Prayer: Almighty God, teach me the importance of prayer in safeguarding my spirit. Help me to cultivate a habit of constant communion with You, drawing strength and guidance from Your presence. Protect me from the enemy's schemes, and lead me in the paths of righteousness. Amen.

DAY 84

THE LEGACY OF HONOR - CARRYING FORWARD THE TRADITIONS OF THOSE WHO SERVED BEFORE US

Scripture: "Remember them which have the rule over you, who have spoken unto you the word of God: whose faith follow, considering the end of their conversation." - Hebrews 13:7 (KJV)

The legacy of honor is built upon the foundation of those who have gone before us, faithfully serving God and country. Just as soldiers honor the traditions of their predecessors, so too must you carry forward the torch of faith and honor. Reflect on Hebrews 13:7, which encourages us to remember and follow the faith of those who have led us. Let the legacy of faithful servants inspire you to walk in their footsteps, upholding the values of honor, integrity, and courage.

Prayer: Gracious Father, thank You for the legacy of faith and honor passed down to us by those who have gone before us. Help me to walk in their footsteps, upholding the traditions of honor and integrity. May my life bring glory to Your name and honor to their memory. Amen.

DAY 85

THE STEADFAST SENTINEL - EMBRACING VIGILANCE AND STEADFASTNESS.

Scripture: "Watch ye, stand fast in the faith, quit you like men, be strong." - 1 Corinthians 16:13 (KJV)

The steadfast sentinel stands guard with vigilance and determination, ever watchful against the schemes of the enemy. Just as soldiers remain vigilant on the battlefield, so too must you stand firm in the faith, unwavering in your commitment to God. Reflect on 1 Corinthians 16:13, which urges us to watch, stand fast in the faith, and be strong. Let vigilance and steadfastness be the hallmarks of your spiritual life, as you remain alert to the attacks of the enemy and resolute in your faith.

Prayer: Almighty God, grant me the strength and vigilance to stand firm in the faith. Help me to be a steadfast sentinel, ever watchful against the schemes of the enemy. May I remain strong and courageous, trusting in Your power to sustain me. Amen.

DAY 86

THE WARRIOR'S RESPITE - FINDING REST AND RENEWAL IN GOD'S PRESENCE

Scripture: "Come unto me, all ye that labour and are heavy laden, and I will give you rest." - Matthew 11:28 (KJV)

The warrior's respite is found in the arms of our Heavenly Father, where we find rest and renewal for our weary souls. Just as soldiers find respite from battle, so too can you find rest in God's presence, laying down your burdens at His feet. Reflect on Matthew 11:28, which invites us to come to Jesus and find rest for our souls. Let His presence be your sanctuary, where you find peace and renewal in the midst of life's challenges.

Prayer: Loving Father, thank You for the rest and renewal found in Your presence. As I come before You, weary and burdened, grant me Your peace that surpasses all understanding. Renew my strength and revive my spirit, that I may continue to walk in Your ways. Amen.

DAY 87

THE TACTICIAN'S TRUTH - ALIGNING STRATEGY WITH SPIRITUAL TRUTH

Scripture: "Thy word is a lamp unto my feet, and a light unto my path." - Psalm 119:105 (KJV)

The tactician's truth is found in aligning strategy with the timeless truths of God's Word. Just as soldiers rely on tactics for victory, so too must you align your plans and strategies with the wisdom found in Scripture. Reflect on Psalm 119:105, which declares that God's Word is a lamp to our feet and a light to our path. Let His Word guide your steps and illuminate your decisions, leading you in the paths of righteousness.

Prayer: Gracious Father, thank You for the truth and wisdom found in Your Word. Help me to align my strategies and plans with Your timeless truths, that I may walk in Your ways and experience Your blessings. Guide me by Your Spirit, and lead me in the paths of righteousness. Amen.

DAY 88
THE HONOR OF HUMBLE SERVICE - SERVING WITH HUMILITY AND HONOR

Scripture: "Let nothing be done through strife or vainglory; but in lowliness of mind let each esteem other better than themselves." - Philippians 2:3 (KJV)

The honor of humble service is found in serving others with humility and selflessness. Just as Jesus humbled Himself to serve others, so too must you follow His example, esteeming others above yourself. Reflect on Philippians 2:3, which urges us to do nothing out of selfish ambition or conceit, but in humility consider others more significant than ourselves. Let humility be the hallmark of your service, as you follow the example of our Lord Jesus Christ.

Prayer: Heavenly Father, teach me the honor of humble service, following the example of Your Son, Jesus Christ. Help me to serve others with humility and selflessness, esteeming them above myself. May my life be a reflection of Your love and grace to those around me. Amen.

DAY 89
THE DISCIPLINE OF THE DEVOUT - CULTIVATING A HEART OF DEVOTION

Scripture: "But thou, when thou prayest, enter into thy closet, and when thou hast shut thy door, pray to thy Father which is in secret; and thy Father which seeth in secret shall reward thee openly." - Matthew 6:6 (KJV)

The discipline of the devout is found in cultivating a heart of devotion through prayer and intimacy with God. Just as soldiers maintain discipline in their training, so too must you cultivate discipline in your spiritual life. Reflect on Matthew 6:6, which encourages us to pray in secret and seek intimacy with God. Let prayer be the cornerstone of your spiritual discipline, as you seek to draw closer to God and deepen your relationship with Him.

Prayer: Gracious Father, grant me the discipline to cultivate a heart of devotion to You. Help me to prioritize prayer and intimacy with

You, knowing that You reward those who seek You in secret. May my life be marked by a deep and abiding relationship with You. Amen.

DAY 90

THE MARCH OF THE FAITHFUL - PERSEVERING IN FAITH THROUGH LIFE'S BATTLES

Scripture: "And let us not be weary in well doing: for in due season we shall reap, if we faint not." - Galatians 6:9 (KJV)

The march of the faithful is marked by perseverance and unwavering faith in God's promises. Just as soldiers press on through fatigue and hardship, so too must you persevere in faith, knowing that God is faithful to fulfil His promises. Reflect on Galatians 6:9, which encourages us not to grow weary in doing good, for in due season we will reap a harvest if we do not give up. Let perseverance be your watchword, as you press on in faith through life's battles.

Prayer: Almighty God, grant me the strength to persevere in faith through life's battles. Help me to trust in Your promises and remain steadfast in Your Word, knowing that You are faithful to fulfill all Your promises. May I never grow weary in doing good, but press on in faith until the end. Amen.

DAY 91

THE SHIELD OF SOLIDARITY - BUILDING BONDS OF FELLOWSHIP AND SUPPORT

Scripture: "Two are better than one; because they have a good reward for their labour. For if they fall, the one will lift up his fellow: but woe to him that is alone when he falleth; for he hath not another to help him up." - Ecclesiastes 4:9-10 (KJV)

The shield of solidarity is forged in the bonds of fellowship and mutual support. Just as soldiers stand shoulder to shoulder in battle, so too must you stand united with your brothers and sisters in Christ, offering encouragement and support in times of need. Reflect on Ecclesiastes 4:9-10, which vividly illustrates the strength found in solidarity and mutual support. Let the bonds of fellowship strengthen you, knowing that together, you can overcome any obstacle that stands in your way.

Prayer: Gracious Father, thank You for the gift of fellowship and support found in the body of Christ. Help me to build strong bonds of solidarity with my brothers and sisters, that we may lift each other up and bear one another's burdens. May our unity bring glory to Your name. Amen.

DAY 92

THE FORTITUDE OF THE FAITHFUL - EMBRACING ENDURANCE IN EVERY ENDEAVOR

Scripture: "And let us not be weary in well doing: for in due season we shall reap, if we faint not." - Galatians 6:9 (KJV)

The fortitude of the faithful is found in enduring steadfastly in every endeavor, trusting in God's promises. Just as soldiers endure hardships on the battlefield, so too must you persevere in faith, knowing that God is faithful to fulfill His promises. Reflect on Galatians 6:9, which encourages us not to grow weary in doing good, for in due season we will reap a harvest if we do not give up. Let perseverance be your watchword, as you press on in faith through life's challenges.

Prayer: Heavenly Father, grant me the fortitude to endure steadfastly in every endeavor. Help me to trust in Your promises and remain faithful in all circumstances, knowing that You are faithful to fulfill Your Word. Strengthen me to press on in faith, knowing that You are with me always. Amen.

DAY 93

THE GUARDIAN'S GRACE - FINDING STRENGTH IN GENTLENESS

Scripture: "But the fruit of the Spirit is love, joy, peace, longsuffering, gentleness, goodness, faith, meekness, temperance: against such there is no law." - Galatians 5:22-23 (KJV)

The guardian's grace is found in strength tempered with gentleness, reflecting the character of Christ. Just as soldiers wield their weapons with precision and control, so too must you exercise strength with gentleness and grace. Reflect on Galatians 5:22-23, which lists gentleness as one of the fruits of the Spirit. Let the grace of gentleness characterize your interactions with others, as you seek to reflect the love and compassion of Christ.

Prayer: Gracious Father, teach me the grace of gentleness, that I may reflect Your character in all that I do. Help me to exercise strength with compassion and grace, showing kindness and gentleness to those around me. May Your love shine through me, bringing glory to Your name. Amen.

DAY 94

THE SOLDIER'S SOLACE - SEEKING COMFORT IN TIMES OF TURMOIL

Scripture: "Cast thy burden upon the Lord, and he shall sustain thee: he shall never suffer the righteous to be moved." - Psalm 55:22 (KJV)

The soldier's solace is found in seeking comfort and refuge in the arms of our Heavenly Father. Just as soldiers find rest in the midst of chaos, so too can you find peace and comfort in God's presence, knowing that He sustains and protects His children. Reflect on Psalm 55:22, which assures us that God will sustain us and never allow the righteous to be moved. Let His promises be your anchor in the storms of life, as you cast your burdens upon Him and find solace in His loving embrace.

Prayer: Loving Father, thank You for being my refuge and strength in times of turmoil. Help me to cast my burdens upon You, knowing that You sustain and protect Your children. May Your peace fill my heart and mind, even in the midst of life's storms. Amen.

DAY 95

THE LEADER'S LEGACY - CRAFTING A LEGACY OF LEADERSHIP AND FAITH

Scripture: "And David shepherded them with integrity of heart; with skillful hands he led them." - Psalm 78:72 (KJV)

The leader's legacy is crafted through leadership guided by integrity and faith. Just as David led with integrity of heart and skillful hands, so too must you lead with wisdom and faithfulness, leaving a legacy that honors God. Reflect on Psalm 78:72, which praises David for his leadership marked by integrity and skill. Let his example inspire you to lead with integrity and faithfulness, knowing that your leadership has the power to impact generations to come.

Prayer: Almighty God, grant me the wisdom and integrity to lead with excellence and faithfulness. Help me to craft a legacy of leadership that honors You and inspires others to follow You wholeheartedly. May my life be a reflection of Your grace and goodness. Amen.

DAY 96

THE WARRIOR'S WORSHIP - HONORING GOD IN THE MIDST OF BATTLE

Scripture: "Sing unto God, sing praises to his name: extol him that rideth upon the heavens by his name Jah, and rejoice before him." - Psalm 68:4 (KJV)

The warrior's worship is a weapon of spiritual warfare, lifting praise and adoration to God in the midst of battle. Just as soldiers rally around their banner in battle, so too must you lift high the banner of praise, declaring the victory that is yours in Christ. Reflect on Psalm 68:4, which exhorts us to sing praises to God's name and rejoice before Him. Let worship be your weapon of choice in spiritual battle, as you declare God's victory and sovereignty over every circumstance.

Prayer: Heavenly Father, I lift my voice in worship and adoration to You, declaring Your greatness and majesty. Thank You for the victory that is mine in Christ. Help me to worship You in spirit and in truth, even in the midst of life's battles. May my worship bring glory to Your name. Amen.

DAY 97

THE DEFENDER'S DUTY - UPHOLDING HONOR AND INTEGRITY

Scripture: "He hath shewed thee, O man, what is good; and what doth the Lord require of thee, but to do justly, and to love mercy, and to walk humbly with thy God?" - Micah 6:8 (KJV)

The defender's duty is to uphold honor and integrity in all things, reflecting the character of our righteous God. Just as soldiers defend their nation's honor on the battlefield, so too must you uphold the honor of God's name in all that you do. Reflect on Micah 6:8, which outlines what the Lord requires of us: to do justly, love mercy, and walk humbly with Him. Let justice, mercy, and humility guide your actions as you fulfill your duty as a defender of the faith.

Prayer: Righteous Father, grant me the strength and courage to uphold honor and integrity in all that I do. Help me to defend Your name and Your truth with boldness and humility, knowing that You are with me always. May my life bring glory to Your name. Amen.

DAY 98

THE CADET'S CALLING - ANSWERING THE CALL TO SERVE WITH CONVICTION

Scripture: "And he said unto them, Go ye into all the world, and preach the gospel to every creature." - Mark 16:15 (KJV)

The cadet's calling is to answer the call to serve with conviction, proclaiming the gospel to a lost and hurting world. Just as soldiers answer the call to duty with courage and determination, so too must you answer the call to share the good news of Jesus Christ with boldness and conviction. Reflect on Mark 16:15, which commands us to go into all the world and preach the gospel to every creature. Let the urgency of the gospel message compel you to action, as you fulfill your calling to be a witness for Christ.

Prayer: Gracious Father, thank You for calling me to be a part of Your kingdom work. Give me boldness and courage to proclaim the gospel to those around me, that they may come to know You as their Lord and Savior. Use me to make a difference in the lives of others. Amen.

DAY 99

THE SENTINEL'S VIGIL - EMBRACING THE WATCHFUL EYE OF FAITH

Scripture: "Watch ye, stand fast in the faith, quit you like men, be strong." - 1 Corinthians 16:13 (KJV)

The sentinel's vigil is marked by watchfulness and faithfulness, standing firm in the face of adversity. Just as soldiers keep watch over their comrades, so too must you keep watch over your soul, remaining steadfast in the faith and vigilant in prayer. Reflect on 1 Corinthians

16:13, which exhorts us to watch, stand fast in the faith, be brave, and be strong. Let faith be your guiding light as you keep watch over your heart and mind, knowing that God is faithful to sustain you.

Prayer: Heavenly Father, help me to be vigilant and watchful in the faith, standing firm against the schemes of the enemy. Grant me strength and courage to persevere in the face of adversity, knowing that You are with me always. May my faith be a beacon of hope to those around me. Amen.

DAY 100
THE CENTURION'S RESOLVE - STANDING FIRM IN CONVICTION AND DUTY

Scripture: "And they said, Believe on the Lord Jesus Christ, and thou shalt be saved, and thy house." - Acts 16:31 (KJV)

The centurion's resolve is to stand firm in conviction and duty, trusting in the saving grace of Jesus Christ. Just as soldiers stand firm in the face of enemy opposition, so too must you stand firm in your faith, knowing that salvation is found in Christ alone. Reflect on Acts 16:31, which promises salvation to all who believe in the Lord Jesus Christ. Let your resolve be unwavering as you trust in the finished work of Christ on the cross, knowing that He has conquered sin and death once and for all.

Prayer: Gracious Savior, thank You for the gift of salvation found in You alone. Give me the resolve to stand firm in conviction and duty, trusting in Your saving grace. May my life be a testimony to Your faithfulness and love. Amen.

DAY 101

THE WARRIOR'S REFLECTION - CONTEMPLATING THE SPIRITUAL LESSONS FROM THE FIELD

Scripture: "I will meditate also of all thy work, and talk of thy doings." - Psalm 77:12 (KJV)

The warrior's reflection is a vital practice, as it allows you to glean spiritual lessons from the battlefield of life. Just as a soldier reflects on past battles to improve tactics, so too must you reflect on your spiritual journey to grow in wisdom and faith. Psalm 77:12 urges us to meditate on God's work and talk of His doings. Take time to reflect on the victories and challenges you've faced, seeking God's guidance and insight in every situation.

Prayer: Gracious Father, grant me the wisdom to reflect on my spiritual journey and learn from both victories and defeats. Help me to discern Your hand at work in every situation, that I may grow in faith and wisdom. Guide my reflections and lead me closer to You. Amen.

DAY 102

THE LEADER'S LAMENT - FINDING STRENGTH
IN MOMENTS OF SORROW

Scripture: "Blessed are they that mourn: for they shall be comforted." - Matthew 5:4 (KJV)

The leader's lament is a testament to the strength found in vulnerability and mourning. Just as a leader acknowledges sorrow, they also find comfort in God's presence and the support of others. In Matthew 5:4, Jesus promises comfort to those who mourn. Embrace your sorrow, for it is through lament that healing begins and strength is renewed.

Prayer: Compassionate Father, in moments of sorrow, grant me Your comforting presence. Help me to find strength in vulnerability and trust in Your promises. May Your peace reign in my heart, even in times of lament. Amen.

DAY 103

THE SOLDIER'S SERENITY - CULTIVATING
INNER PEACE AMIDST OUTER TURMOIL

Scripture: "And the peace of God, which passeth all understanding, shall keep your hearts and minds through Christ Jesus." - Philippians 4:7 (KJV)

The soldier's serenity is found in cultivating inner peace amidst the chaos of life. Just as a soldier remains calm under fire, so too must you find peace in God's presence, knowing that He is in control. Philippians 4:7 assures us of the peace that surpasses understanding, guarding our hearts and minds in Christ Jesus. Seek this peace through prayer and trust in God's sovereignty.

Prayer: Prince of Peace, grant me Your serenity in the midst of life's storms. Help me to trust in Your sovereignty and find peace in Your presence. Guard my heart and mind, that I may remain steadfast in faith. Amen.

DAY 104
THE DEFENDER'S DEVOTION - COMMITTING TO A CAUSE GREATER THAN ONESELF

Scripture: "Greater love hath no man than this, that a man lay down his life for his friends." - John 15:13 (KJV)

The defender's devotion is rooted in sacrificial love and commitment to a cause greater than oneself. Just as a defender lays down their life for others, so too must you devote yourself wholeheartedly to God's kingdom work. John 15:13 exemplifies this sacrificial love. Surrender your life to God's service, knowing that true fulfillment comes from serving others in His name.

Prayer: Loving Father, ignite in me a spirit of sacrificial devotion to Your kingdom work. Help me to lay down my life for others as You laid down Yours for me. May Your love compel me to serve with joy and dedication. Amen.

DAY 105

THE CADET'S CURIOSITY - FOSTERING A SPIRIT OF LEARNING AND GROWTH

Scripture: "Give instruction to a wise man, and he will be yet wiser: teach a just man, and he will increase in learning." - Proverbs 9:9 (KJV)

The cadet's curiosity fuels a desire for learning and growth. Just as a cadet seeks knowledge to excel in their training, so too must you cultivate a teachable spirit to grow in wisdom and understanding. Proverbs 9:9 emphasizes the value of instruction and learning. Embrace opportunities for growth, knowing that each lesson brings you closer to fulfilling God's purpose for your life.

Prayer: Wise Teacher, grant me a hunger for learning and a thirst for wisdom. Help me to approach each day with curiosity and humility, eager to grow in knowledge and understanding. Guide me in Your truth and light. Amen.

DAY 106

THE GUARDIAN'S LOYALTY - UPHOLDING THE VALUES OF SERVICE AND FIDELITY

Scripture: "Let love and faithfulness never leave you; bind them around your neck, write them on the tablet of your heart." - Proverbs 3:3 (KJV)

The guardian's loyalty is anchored in love and faithfulness, embodying the values of service and fidelity. Just as a guardian remains steadfast in their duties, so too must you uphold the principles of love and faithfulness in all areas of life. Proverbs 3:3 encourages us to let love and faithfulness guide our actions. Embrace these virtues as you serve others with unwavering loyalty and devotion.

Prayer: Faithful Guardian, instill in me a heart of love and faithfulness to serve You and others with unwavering loyalty. May Your values be written on my heart, guiding me in all that I do. Help me to reflect Your love to the world. Amen.

DAY 107

THE CENTURION'S CLARITY - LEADING WITH CLEAR PURPOSE AND VISION

Scripture: "For God is not the author of confusion, but of peace, as in all churches of the saints." - 1 Corinthians 14:33 (KJV)

The centurion's clarity is characterized by clear purpose and vision, guided by God's peace. Just as a centurion leads with confidence and direction, so too must you seek clarity in your leadership, trusting in God's guidance. 1 Corinthians 14:33 reminds us that God is not the author of confusion but of peace. Seek His wisdom and direction, that your leadership may bring clarity and peace to those you serve.

Prayer: Sovereign God, grant me clarity of purpose and vision as I lead others. Help me to seek Your wisdom and guidance in all decisions, trusting in Your peace to guide my steps. May Your will be done in and through me. Amen.

DAY 108
THE WARRIOR'S HARMONY - BALANCING STRENGTH WITH COMPASSION

Scripture: "And above all these things put on charity, which is the bond of perfectness." - Colossians 3:14 (KJV)

The warrior's harmony is found in balancing strength with compassion, embodying the virtue of charity. Just as a warrior wields strength in battle, so too must you exercise compassion and love in all interactions. Colossians 3:14 exhorts us to put on charity, which binds all virtues together in perfect harmony. Seek this balance in your life, knowing that true strength is found in love.

Prayer: Merciful Savior, teach me to balance strength with compassion, that I may reflect Your love to the world. Help me to clothe myself in charity, the bond of perfectness, as I navigate life's challenges. May Your grace abound in me. Amen.

DAY 109
THE LEADER'S LEARNING - EMBRACING CONTINUOUS GROWTH AND KNOWLEDGE

Scripture: "But grow in grace, and in the knowledge of our Lord and Saviour Jesus Christ. To him be glory both now and for ever. Amen." - 2 Peter 3:18 (KJV)

The leader's learning is marked by continuous growth and knowledge, rooted in grace and the study of God's Word. Just as a leader seeks to improve and develop, so too must you pursue spiritual growth and understanding. 2 Peter 3:18 encourages us to grow in grace and in the knowledge of our Lord and Savior Jesus Christ. Commit yourself to lifelong learning and growth, knowing that it brings glory to God.

Prayer: Gracious God, grant me a hunger for Your Word and a thirst for knowledge. Help me to grow in grace and understanding, that I may lead others with wisdom and humility. Guide me in Your truth. Amen.

DAY 110

THE SOLDIER'S STEADINESS - STANDING FIRM IN FAITH THROUGH LIFE'S STORMS

Scripture: "Watch ye, stand fast in the faith, quit you like men, be strong." - 1 Corinthians 16:13 (KJV)

The soldier's steadiness is demonstrated by standing firm in faith amidst life's storms. Just as a soldier remains steadfast under fire, so too must you stand strong in your faith, trusting in God's unfailing promises. 1 Corinthians 16:13 exhorts us to watch, stand fast in the faith, be brave, and be strong. Anchor yourself in God's Word and truth, knowing that He is your rock and refuge in every trial.

Prayer: Mighty Fortress, grant me the strength and courage to stand firm in faith, even in the midst of life's storms. Help me to trust in Your unfailing promises and remain steadfast in Your love. May Your grace sustain me. Amen.

DAY 111

THE DEFENDER'S DETERMINATION - PURSUING JUSTICE WITH UNWAVERING RESOLVE

Scripture: "He hath shewed thee, O man, what is good; and what doth the LORD require of thee, but to do justly, and to love mercy, and to walk humbly with thy God?" - Micah 6:8 (KJV)

The defender's determination is rooted in the pursuit of justice with unwavering resolve. Just as a defender stands firm in the face of adversity, so too must you uphold righteousness and seek justice with courage and determination. Micah 6:8 reminds us of God's requirements: to do justly, love mercy, and walk humbly with Him. Let this verse guide your actions as you strive to make a difference in the world.

Prayer: Heavenly Father, grant me the strength and determination to pursue justice with unwavering resolve. Help me to stand firm in righteousness and uphold Your standards of truth and fairness. May Your will be done on earth as it is in heaven. Amen.

DAY 112
THE CADET'S CREATIVITY - INNOVATING WITHIN THE TRADITIONS OF MILITARY EXCELLENCE

Scripture: "Behold, I will do a new thing; now it shall spring forth; shall ye not know it? I will even make a way in the wilderness, and rivers in the desert." - Isaiah 43:19 (KJV)

The cadet's creativity is found in innovating within the traditions of military excellence. Just as a cadet embraces new strategies while honoring the wisdom of the past, so too must you cultivate a spirit of creativity and innovation in all aspects of life. Isaiah 43:19 speaks of

God's ability to do new things and make a way where there seems to be none. Let this verse inspire you to think outside the box and seek new solutions to old problems.

Prayer: Gracious God, ignite in me a spirit of creativity and innovation as I navigate the challenges of life. Help me to honor tradition while embracing new ideas and strategies. Guide me in paths of righteousness and wisdom. Amen.

DAY 113
THE BRIGADIER'S BALANCE - MASTERING THE EQUILIBRIUM OF DUTY AND FAITH

Scripture: "But seek ye first the kingdom of God, and his righteousness; and all these things shall be added unto you." - Matthew 6:33 (KJV)

The brigadier's balance is found in mastering the equilibrium of duty and faith. Just as a brigadier prioritizes responsibilities while seeking God's guidance, so too must you seek first the kingdom of God in all that you do. Matthew 6:33 teaches us to prioritize God's kingdom and righteousness above all else. Let this verse remind you of the importance of maintaining balance and perspective in life, trusting that God will provide for your needs.

Prayer: Heavenly Father, help me to maintain balance in my life, prioritizing Your kingdom and righteousness above all else. Grant me wisdom to fulfill my duties faithfully while keeping my eyes fixed on You. May Your will be done in my life. Amen.

DAY 114
THE ENSIGN'S ENLIGHTENMENT - SEEKING WISDOM THROUGH SPIRITUAL DISCIPLINE

Scripture: "If any of you lack wisdom, let him ask of God, that giveth to all men liberally, and upbraideth not; and it shall be given him." - James 1:5 (KJV)

The ensign's enlightenment is found in seeking wisdom through spiritual discipline. Just as an ensign train diligently to excel in their duties, so too must you pursue wisdom through prayer, study, and obedience to God's Word. James 1:5 assures us that God generously gives wisdom to those who ask. Let this verse encourage you to seek God's wisdom in all areas of life, knowing that He will guide and enlighten you.

Prayer: Gracious God, grant me wisdom as I seek to navigate the challenges of life. Help me to cultivate spiritual discipline and seek Your guidance in all that I do. Open my eyes to Your truth and enlighten my understanding. Amen.

DAY 115

THE TROOPER'S TRANQUILITY - CULTIVATING INNER PEACE AMIDST EXTERNAL PRESSURES

Scripture: "Peace I leave with you, my peace I give unto you: not as the world giveth, give I unto you. Let not your heart be troubled, neither let it be afraid." - John 14:27 (KJV)

The trooper's tranquility is found in cultivating inner peace amidst external pressures. Just as a trooper remains calm under fire, so too must you receive and embrace the peace that Christ offers, even in the midst of life's storms. John 14:27 reminds us of Jesus' promise of peace, a peace that surpasses understanding and transcends worldly circumstances. Let this verse anchor your soul in times of trouble, trusting in God's sovereignty and love.

Prayer: Prince of Peace, grant me Your tranquility in the midst of life's storms. Help me to rest in Your peace, knowing that You are in control. Calm my troubled heart and fill me with Your presence. Amen.

DAY 116
THE MARSHAL'S MERCY - EXERCISING COMPASSION IN COMMAND

Scripture: "But love ye your enemies, and do good, and lend, hoping for nothing again; and your reward shall be great, and ye shall be the children of the Highest: for he is kind unto the unthankful and to the evil." - Luke 6:35 (KJV)

The marshal's mercy is found in exercising compassion in command. Just as a marshal shows kindness and mercy to those under their authority, so too must you extend grace and compassion to others, even in positions of leadership. Luke 6:35 encourages us to love our enemies, do good to them, and lend without expecting anything in return. Let this verse inspire you to lead with kindness and mercy, reflecting God's love to all.

Prayer: Compassionate Father, grant me a heart of mercy and kindness as I lead and serve others. Help me to show grace and compassion to those under my authority, reflecting Your love and mercy. May Your kindness shine through me. Amen.

DAY 117
THE SQUADRON'S SPIRIT - FOSTERING UNITY AND FELLOWSHIP IN SERVICE

Scripture: "Behold, how good and how pleasant it is for brethren to dwell together in unity!" - Psalm 133:1 (KJV)

The squadron's spirit is found in fostering unity and fellowship in service. Just as a squadron works together as a cohesive unit, so too must you cultivate unity and harmony among fellow believers, serving together in love and fellowship. Psalm 133:1 celebrates the beauty of unity among brethren. Let this verse inspire you to pursue peace and unity in all your relationships, knowing that it pleases God and strengthens His church.

Prayer: Gracious God, unite us as one body, bound together in love and fellowship. Help us to work together in harmony, serving You and one another with joy and dedication. May Your Spirit guide us in unity and peace. Amen.

DAY 118
THE RECRUIT'S RESOLVE - EMBRACING THE JOURNEY FROM NOVICE TO EXPERT

Scripture: "And he said unto me, My grace is sufficient for thee: for my strength is made perfect in weakness. Most gladly therefore will I rather glory in my infirmities, that the power of Christ may rest upon me." - 2 Corinthians 12:9 (KJV)

The recruit's resolve is found in embracing the journey from novice to expert. Just as a recruit undergoes training and growth to become a skilled soldier, so too must you embrace the process of spiritual growth and maturity, knowing that God's grace is sufficient for every step of the journey. 2 Corinthians 12:9 reminds us that God's strength is made perfect in our weakness. Let this verse encourage you to press on in faith, trusting that God will empower you to overcome every obstacle and grow in Him.

Prayer: Sovereign Lord, strengthen me in my journey of faith, from novice to expert. Help me to embrace the challenges and trials that come my way, knowing that Your grace is always sufficient. May Your power be made perfect in my weakness. Amen.

DAY 119
THE VETERAN'S VALOR - HONORING THE SPIRITUAL BATTLES AND TRIUMPHS OF SERVICE

Scripture: "Fight the good fight of faith, lay hold on eternal life, whereunto thou art also called, and hast professed a good profession before many witnesses." - 1 Timothy 6:12 (KJV)

The veteran's valor is found in honoring the spiritual battles and triumphs of service. Just as a veteran reflects on past battles and victories, so too must you remember and celebrate the faithfulness of God in your life, acknowledging His provision and protection. 1 Timothy 6:12 encourages us to fight the good fight of faith and lay hold on eternal life. Let this verse inspire you to persevere in your spiritual journey, knowing that God is faithful to fulfill His promises to you.

Prayer: Almighty God, thank You for Your faithfulness throughout my journey of faith. Strengthen me with Your Spirit as I continue to fight the good fight and lay hold on eternal life. May Your name be glorified in all I do. Amen.

DAY 120
THE DRILLMASTER'S DISCIPLINE - EMBRACING THE RIGOR OF SPIRITUAL PRACTICE

Scripture: "And every man that striveth for the mastery is temperate in all things. Now they do it to obtain a corruptible crown; but we an incorruptible." - 1 Corinthians 9:25 (KJV)

The drillmaster's discipline is found in embracing the rigor of spiritual practice. Just as a drillmaster trains soldiers with discipline and dedication, so too must you cultivate spiritual disciplines such as prayer, fasting, and studying God's Word, knowing that they lead to spiritual growth and maturity. 1 Corinthians 9:25 compares the

Christian life to an athlete striving for mastery. Let this verse encourage you to be disciplined in your spiritual practices, knowing that the rewards of faith far outweigh any temporal rewards.

Prayer: Gracious Father, help me to embrace the discipline of spiritual practice, knowing that it leads to spiritual growth and maturity. Guide me in cultivating habits of prayer, fasting, and study, that I may grow closer to You each day. Amen.

DAY 121
THE NAVIGATOR'S NORTH STAR - FINDING GUIDANCE IN FAITH DURING UNCERTAIN TIMES

Scripture: "Thy word is a lamp unto my feet, and a light unto my path." - Psalm 119:105 (KJV)

In the vast expanse of life's uncertainties, your faith serves as the North Star guiding you through the darkest nights and the stormiest seas. Just as a navigator relies on the constancy of the North Star for direction, so too must you anchor your soul in the unchanging truth of God's Word. Psalm 119:105 reminds us that God's Word illuminates our path, providing guidance and clarity in times of confusion and doubt. Let His Word be your constant companion, lighting the way through every trial and tribulation.

Prayer: Heavenly Father, in the midst of life's uncertainties, I look to You as my guiding North Star. Illuminate my path with Your Word, that I may walk in confidence and faith. Lead me through the storms of life, and may Your presence be my constant comfort and guide. Amen.

DAY 122
THE ARTISAN'S CRAFT - HONING THE SOUL WITH THE PRECISION OF A SKILLED CRAFTSPERSON

Scripture: "But now, O Lord, thou art our father; we are the clay, and thou our potter; and we all are the work of thy hand." - Isaiah 64:8 (KJV)

Just as an artisan crafts a masterpiece with skill and precision, so too does God shape and mold your soul with loving care and attention. Surrender to His hands, for He is the master craftsman, shaping you into a vessel of beauty and purpose. Isaiah 64:8 illustrates God's role as the potter and humanity as the clay. Allow Him to mold you according to His divine design, trusting that His craftsmanship will result in a life of significance and fulfillment.

Prayer: Gracious God, shape me according to Your will, for You are the master craftsman of my soul. Mold me with Your loving hands, that I may reflect Your beauty and glory in all that I do. May my life be a masterpiece of Your grace and mercy. Amen.

DAY 123
THE MEDIC'S MISSION - HEALING HEARTS AND SPIRITS WITH COMPASSION

Scripture: "He healeth the broken in heart, and bindeth up their wounds." - Psalm 147:3 (KJV)

As a medic tends to physical wounds, so too must you minister to the brokenness of the heart and spirit with compassion and empathy. Embrace your mission with tenderness, for in comforting others, you reflect the love and compassion of the Great Physician. Psalm 147:3 reassures us of God's healing touch upon the brokenhearted. Let His example inspires you to extend comfort and healing to those who are hurting, offering solace and hope in times of despair.

Prayer: Compassionate Father, grant me a heart of compassion to minister to the wounded and brokenhearted. Use me as Your instrument of healing and restoration, bringing comfort and peace to those in need. May Your love shine through me as I extend Your healing touch to others. Amen.

DAY 124
THE PILOT'S PERSPECTIVE - GAINING A
HIGHER VIEW ON LIFE'S CHALLENGES

Scripture: "But they that wait upon the Lord shall renew their strength; they shall mount up with wings as eagles; they shall run, and not be weary; and they shall walk, and not faint." - Isaiah 40:31 (KJV)

Like a pilot soaring above the clouds, rise above life's challenges and gain a heavenly perspective. As you wait upon the Lord, He will renew your strength, enabling you to navigate life's turbulence with courage and endurance. Isaiah 40:31 promises that those who wait upon the Lord will soar on wings like eagles. Let this verse remind you of the power of God to lift you above life's trials and give you a renewed perspective on His faithfulness.

Prayer: Sovereign Lord, grant me the perspective of a pilot soaring above the storms of life. Renew my strength as I wait upon You, that I may rise above every challenge with faith and courage. Help me to trust in Your provision and guidance. Amen.

DAY 125

THE ENGINEER'S INGENUITY - BUILDING
BRIDGES TO SPIRITUAL UNDERSTANDING

Scripture: "Study to shew thyself approved unto God, a workman that needeth not to be ashamed, rightly dividing the word of truth."
- 2 Timothy 2:15 (KJV)

Just as an engineer designs and constructs bridges, so too must you build bridges to spiritual understanding through diligent study and discernment of God's Word. Be a workman who rightly divides the word of truth, bringing clarity and insight to those seeking answers. 2 Timothy 2:15 encourages us to study diligently to show ourselves approved unto God. Let this verse inspire you to delve deep into the Scriptures, seeking wisdom and understanding from the Author of life.

Prayer: Heavenly Father, grant me wisdom and discernment as I study Your Word. Help me to rightly divide the truth and build bridges to spiritual understanding. May Your Word be a lamp unto my feet and a light unto my path. Amen.

DAY 126

THE SCOUT'S SURVEY - EXPLORING THE TERRAIN OF THE SOUL WITH CURIOSITY

Scripture: "Search me, O God, and know my heart: try me, and know my thoughts: And see if there be any wicked way in me, and lead me in the way everlasting." - Psalm 139:23-24 (KJV)

As a scout surveys the land, explore the terrain of your soul with curiosity and openness before God. Invite Him to search your heart, revealing any hidden motives or desires, that He may lead you in the way everlasting. Psalm 139:23-24 is a prayer of surrender, inviting God to search our hearts and lead us in His ways. Let this prayer guide you in your journey of self-discovery and spiritual growth.

Prayer: Gracious God, search my heart and know my thoughts. Reveal to me any areas of my life that are not aligned with Your will. Lead me in the way everlasting, that I may walk in obedience and faithfulness before You. Amen.

DAY 127

THE ARTISAN'S ACCURACY - PRECISION AND CARE IN EVERY SPIRITUAL ENDEAVOR

Scripture: "And whatsoever ye do, do it heartily, as to the Lord, and not unto men." - Colossians 3:23 (KJV)

Like an artisan who crafts with precision and care, approach every spiritual endeavor with diligence and excellence, knowing that you serve the Lord in all that you do. Let your actions reflect the accuracy and attention to detail that honor God and bless others. Colossians 3:23 reminds us to do everything heartily, as unto the Lord. Let this verse inspire you to pursue excellence in your spiritual walk, knowing that your efforts are not in vain before the eyes of the Lord.

Prayer: Heavenly Father, grant me the diligence and precision of an artisan in all my spiritual endeavors. Help me to serve You wholeheartedly, with excellence and care. May my life be a reflection of Your glory and grace. Amen.

DAY 128
THE NAVIGATOR'S FORESIGHT - ANTICIPATING CHALLENGES WITH WISDOM

Scripture: "A prudent man foreseeth the evil, and hideth himself: but the simple pass on, and are punished." - Proverbs 22:3 (KJV)

Like a navigator who anticipates storms on the horizon, cultivate foresight and wisdom to navigate life's challenges with discernment and insight. Be prudent in your decisions, seeking God's guidance to avoid pitfalls and dangers along the way. Proverbs 22:3 highlights the importance of foresight in avoiding trouble. Let this verse encourage you to seek wisdom from God, that you may navigate life's journey with discernment and discretion.

Prayer: Sovereign Lord, grant me the wisdom and foresight to anticipate challenges and obstacles on my journey. Guide me in making prudent decisions that honor You and lead to life and blessing. May Your Spirit be my constant companion and guide. Amen.

DAY 129

THE SENTINEL'S INSIGHT - DISCERNING TRUTH IN A COMPLEX WORLD

Scripture: "Beloved, believe not every spirit, but try the spirits whether they are of God: because many false prophets are gone out into the world." - 1 John 4:1 (KJV)

As a sentinel stands watch, discern truth from falsehood in a world filled with deception and confusion. Test every spirit against the truth of God's Word, for many false prophets seek to lead astray. Be vigilant in guarding your heart and mind against deception. 1 John 4:1 admonishes us to test the spirits to see if they are from God. Let this verse remind you to exercise discernment and wisdom in discerning truth from error, relying on the guidance of the Holy Spirit.

Prayer: Gracious Father, grant me discernment and insight to distinguish truth from falsehood in a world filled with deception. Help me to test every spirit against the truth of Your Word, that I may walk in wisdom and discernment. May Your Spirit guide me in all things. Amen.

DAY 130

EMBRACING COURAGE IN THE FACE OF UNCERTAINTY

Scripture: "Be strong and of a good courage, fear not, nor be afraid of them: for the Lord thy God, he it is that doth go with thee; he will not fail thee, nor forsake thee." - Deuteronomy 31:6 (KJV)

In the face of uncertainty, take courage and trust in the Lord who goes before you. Fear not, for He is with you, guiding and sustaining you through every trial and tribulation. Let His presence be your source of courage and strength. Deuteronomy 31:6 assures us of God's faithfulness and presence in times of uncertainty. Let this verse embolden you to face each day with courage and confidence, knowing that God goes before you.

Prayer: Heavenly Father, in times of uncertainty, grant me courage and strength to trust in Your unfailing promises. Help me to fear not, knowing that You are with me always. May Your presence be my constant comfort and assurance. Amen.

DAY 131
THE POWER OF PRAYER IN COMBAT ZONES

Scripture: "Be careful for nothing; but in everything by prayer and supplication with thanksgiving let your requests be made known unto God." - Philippians 4:6 (KJV)

In the heat of battle, amidst the chaos and danger, the power of prayer becomes a steadfast anchor for the soul. Philippians 4:6 reminds us that in every situation, we can turn to God in prayer, laying our burdens before Him with thanksgiving. Just as David prayed fervently before facing Goliath and Jehoshaphat sought God's guidance before battle, so too must you engage in earnest prayer in combat zones. Your prayers connect you to the Almighty, who is your refuge and strength in times of trouble.

Prayer: Gracious God, in the midst of the battlefield, we seek Your presence and protection. Hear our prayers as we cry out to You for strength, courage, and guidance. May Your peace reign in our hearts, and may Your divine power sustain us through every trial. Amen.

DAY 132
FINDING PEACE IN THE MIDST OF CHAOS

Scripture: "Peace I leave with you, my peace I give unto you: not as the world giveth, give I unto you. Let not your heart be troubled, neither let it be afraid." - John 14:27 (KJV)

In the turmoil and tumult of life's storms, Jesus offers a peace that transcends understanding. John 14:27 assures us of the peace that comes from Him, a peace that calms our troubled hearts and soothes our fears. Like Jesus sleeping peacefully amidst the raging storm on the Sea of Galilee, so too can you find peace in the midst of chaos by resting in His presence. Trust in His promises, knowing that He is in control and will never leave nor forsake you.

Prayer: Prince of Peace, in the midst of life's storms, we seek Your calming presence. Quiet our anxious hearts and still our troubled minds with Your perfect peace. Help us to trust in Your unfailing love and to find refuge in Your mighty arms. Amen.

DAY 133
THE ARMOR OF FAITH: PROTECTING YOUR SPIRIT

Scripture: "Put on the whole armour of God, that ye may be able to stand against the wiles of the devil." - Ephesians 6:11 (KJV)

In the spiritual warfare that surrounds you, the armor of faith becomes your shield and protection. Ephesians 6:11 exhorts you to put on the whole armor of God, equipping yourself to stand firm against the schemes of the enemy. Just as a soldier dons' physical armor before entering battle, so too must you clothe yourself in the spiritual armor of truth, righteousness, peace, faith, salvation, and the Word of God.

This armor empowers you to resist the attacks of the evil one and to stand firm in your faith.

Prayer: Heavenly Father, clothe us with Your armor of faith, that we may stand strong against the spiritual forces of darkness. Guard our hearts and minds with Your truth and righteousness. May Your Word be a lamp unto our feet and a light unto our path. Amen.

DAY 134
LEADERSHIP AND WISDOM FROM BIBLICAL WARRIORS

Scripture: "And David behaved himself wisely in all his ways; and the Lord was with him." - 1 Samuel 18:14 (KJV)

The pages of Scripture are filled with stories of courageous warriors who led with wisdom and discernment. David, Joshua, and Deborah are just a few examples of biblical leaders who sought God's guidance and led their people with integrity and courage. In the footsteps of these great leaders, you too are called to lead with wisdom and discernment. Seek God's guidance in all your ways, trusting that He will direct your steps and give you the wisdom to lead effectively.

Prayer: Almighty God, grant us the wisdom and discernment of biblical warriors, that we may lead with integrity and courage. Guide our steps and direct our paths as we seek to follow Your will. May Your Spirit empower us to lead with humility and grace. Amen.

DAY 135

OVERCOMING FEAR WITH DIVINE STRENGTH

Scripture: "For God hath not given us the spirit of fear; but of power, and of love, and of a sound mind." - 2 Timothy 1:7 (KJV)

Fear is a natural response to the uncertainties of life, but as a child of God, you are called to overcome fear with divine strength. 2 Timothy 1:7 reminds you that God has not given you a spirit of fear, but of power, love, and a sound mind. Just as Joshua found courage in God's promises as he led the Israelites into the Promised Land, so too can you draw strength from God's presence and promises. Trust in His unfailing love and mighty power to overcome every fear that threatens to hold you captive.

Prayer: Sovereign Lord, banish the spirit of fear from our hearts and minds, and fill us with Your divine strength and courage. Help us to trust in Your promises and to walk boldly in the power of Your Spirit. May Your love cast out all fear and bring us peace. Amen.

DAY 136

THE SOLDIER'S PSALM: A DAILY SHIELD

Scripture: "The Lord is my rock, and my fortress, and my deliverer; my God, my strength, in whom I will trust; my buckler, and the horn of my salvation, and my high tower." - Psalm 18:2 (KJV)

In the midst of life's battles, the Soldier's Psalm becomes a daily shield of protection and strength. Psalm 18:2 declares the Lord as your rock, fortress, deliverer, strength, buckler, salvation, and high tower, a refuge and stronghold in times of trouble. As you meditate on the truths of Psalm 18, let it be a source of comfort and courage, reminding you of God's faithfulness and power to save. Take refuge in His presence, knowing that He is your ultimate defender and protector.

Prayer: Gracious Father, thank You for being our rock, fortress, and deliverer in times of trouble. May the truths of Psalm 18 be a source of strength and comfort to us each day. Help us to trust in Your unfailing love and to take refuge in Your mighty arms. Amen.

DAY 137
BUILDING RESILIENCE THROUGH SPIRITUAL ENDURANCE

Scripture: "But he that shall endure unto the end, the same shall be saved." - Matthew 24:13 (KJV)

In the face of adversity and trials, spiritual endurance becomes the cornerstone of resilience. Matthew 24:13 reminds you of the importance of enduring to the end, for it is through endurance that you will find salvation and victory. Just as the apostle Paul endured hardships and persecution for the sake of the gospel, so too must you persevere in faith, knowing that God is faithful to sustain you through every trial. Cultivate spiritual endurance through prayer, meditation on God's Word, and fellowship with fellow believers.

Prayer: Heavenly Father, grant us the strength and endurance to persevere in faith, even in the midst of trials and tribulations. Help us to fix our eyes on Jesus, the author and finisher of our faith, knowing that our endurance will lead to salvation and eternal life. Amen.

DAY 138
NAVIGATING MORAL DILEMMAS WITH GOD'S GUIDANCE

Scripture: "Trust in the Lord with all thine heart; and lean not unto thine own understanding. In all thy ways acknowledge him, and he shall direct thy paths." - Proverbs 3:5-6 (KJV)

When faced with moral dilemmas and difficult decisions, trust in the Lord and seek His guidance. Proverbs 3:5-6 reminds you to lean not on your own understanding but to acknowledge God in all your ways, trusting that He will direct your paths. Like Daniel, who refused to compromise his faith and integrity despite facing dire consequences, so too must you seek God's wisdom and guidance in navigating moral dilemmas. Trust in His promises to lead and guide you, knowing that He will never leave nor forsake you.

Prayer: Gracious God, grant us wisdom and discernment as we navigate moral dilemmas and difficult decisions. Help us to trust in Your guidance and to lean not on our own understanding. May Your Spirit lead us in paths of righteousness and truth. Amen.

DAY 139
THE FELLOWSHIP OF SERVICE: UNITY IN FAITH

Scripture: "For as we have many members in one body, and all members have not the same office: So we, being many, are one body in Christ, and every one members one of another." - Romans 12:4-5 (KJV)

As members of the body of Christ, you are called to serve one another in love and unity. Romans 12:4-5 reminds you that though you may have different gifts and roles, you are all part of the same body, united in Christ. Just as soldiers in a unit work together towards a common mission, so too must you join together in fellowship and service, supporting and encouraging one another in the faith. Let love and unity characterize your relationships, reflecting the love of Christ to the world.

Prayer: Heavenly Father, unite us as one body in Christ, bound together by love and faith. Help us to serve one another in humility and grace, bearing each other's burdens and sharing in each other's joys. May Your love be the bond of our fellowship, bringing glory to Your name. Amen.

DAY 140

HEALING FROM LOSS: COMFORT IN SCRIPTURE

Scripture: "He healeth the broken in heart, and bindeth up their wounds." - Psalm 147:3 (KJV)

In times of loss and grief, find comfort and healing in the promises of Scripture. Psalm 147:3 assures you that God heals the brokenhearted and binds up their wounds, offering solace and restoration in the midst of pain. Like Jesus, who wept with Mary and Martha at the death of Lazarus, so too does God empathize with your sorrow and grief. Turn to Him in prayer and meditation on His Word, finding comfort in His loving presence and promises of eternal life.

Prayer: Compassionate God, we come to You with broken hearts, seeking Your comfort and healing in times of loss and grief. Heal our wounds and bind up our brokenness, Lord, that we may find peace and solace in Your loving arms. May Your presence bring us hope and strength to face each day. Amen.

DAY 141

MARCHING WITH MERCY: EXTENDING FORGIVENESS IN THE FIELD

Scripture: "Be ye therefore merciful, as your Father also is merciful." - Luke 6:36 (KJV)

In the battlefield of life, the command to march with mercy resonates deeply. Luke 6:36 reminds you of the profound mercy of God and calls you to extend that same mercy to others. Just as God forgives you, He expects you to forgive others, even in the midst of conflict and struggle. Forgiveness is not weakness but rather a display of spiritual strength and maturity. Just as Joseph forgave his brothers who sold him into slavery, and as Jesus forgave those who crucified Him, so too are you called to forgive those who have wronged you.

Prayer: Heavenly Father, grant me the strength to march with mercy, extending forgiveness to those who have wronged me. Help me to emulate Your boundless mercy and to show compassion to others, even in difficult circumstances. May Your grace empower me to walk in forgiveness each day. Amen.

DAY 142

THE STRENGTH OF SILENCE: LISTENING FOR GOD'S VOICE

Scripture: "Be still, and know that I am God..." - Psalm 46:10 (KJV)Y

In the cacophony of life, finding strength in silence is essential. Psalm 46:10 calls you to be still and recognize the presence of God. In the quietness of your heart, you can hear His voice and discern His will. Just as Elijah heard God's whisper in the stillness after the storm, so too can you experience His guidance and reassurance when you quiet your soul before Him. Silence is not empty; it is filled with the presence of God, speaking peace and wisdom to your spirit.

Prayer: Gracious God, in the busyness of life, grant me the discipline to be still and listen for Your voice. Help me to find strength and guidance in the silence of Your presence. Speak to my heart, Lord, and lead me in the way everlasting. Amen.

DAY 143

WARRIOR WOMEN OF THE BIBLE: LESSONS OF BRAVERY

Scripture: "She is clothed with strength and dignity, and she laughs without fear of the future." - Proverbs 31:25 (NLT)

The Bible is replete with examples of courageous women who embodied strength and bravery. From Deborah, who led Israel fearlessly into battle, to Esther, who risked her life to save her people, these women inspire you to embrace bravery in every aspect of life. Just as Jael used her wit and courage to defeat Israel's enemies, so too can you tap into the strength and courage that God has placed within you. As you study their lives, you'll discover that true bravery comes from trusting in God's power and provision.

Prayer: Sovereign Lord, thank You for the examples of brave women in Your Word. Help me to cultivate courage and strength in my own life, trusting in Your power to sustain me. May I walk in the footsteps of these courageous women, fearless and full of faith. Amen.

DAY 144
DAILY GRATITUDE: COUNTING BLESSINGS IN SERVICE

Scripture: "Give thanks in all circumstances; for this is God's will for you in Christ Jesus." - 1 Thessalonians 5:18

In the midst of your service, cultivate a heart of gratitude. 1 Thessalonians 5:18 encourages you to give thanks in all circumstances, recognizing that every blessing comes from God's hand. Whether in times of triumph or trial, there is always something to be grateful for. As you count your blessings, you'll find that gratitude fills your heart with joy and contentment, even amidst the challenges of service.

Prayer: Gracious God, teach me to cultivate a heart of gratitude in all circumstances. Help me to recognize Your blessings in my life, both big and small. May my heart overflow with thanksgiving as I serve You and others with joy. Amen.

DAY 145
THE DISCIPLINE OF DEVOTION: STAYING SPIRITUALLY FIT

Scripture: "But seek ye first the kingdom of God, and his righteousness; and all these things shall be added unto you." - Matthew 6:33 (KJV)

Just as physical fitness requires discipline and commitment, so too does spiritual fitness. Matthew 6:33 reminds you to prioritize seeking God's kingdom and righteousness above all else. Devotion is not merely a one-time commitment but a daily discipline of seeking God through prayer, Scripture, worship, and service. Like athletes training for a race, invest time and effort into your spiritual growth, knowing that it yields eternal rewards.

Prayer: Heavenly Father, help me to prioritize seeking Your kingdom and righteousness above all else. Grant me the discipline and devotion to stay spiritually fit, that I may grow in intimacy with You and be effective in Your service. May my life be a testament to Your grace and power. Amen.

DAY 146

SERVING WITH HONOR: UPHOLDING INTEGRITY UNDER PRESSURE

Scripture: "The integrity of the upright shall guide them: but the perverseness of transgressors shall destroy them." - Proverbs 11:3 (KJV)

In the face of pressure and temptation, uphold integrity in your service. Proverbs 11:3 affirms that the integrity of the upright guides them, while dishonesty leads to destruction. Just as Daniel remained faithful to God's commands despite facing the lion's den, so too must you maintain integrity in all your dealings. Let honesty and righteousness be the hallmarks of your service, reflecting the character of Christ to the world.

Prayer: Gracious God, grant me the strength and courage to serve with honor, upholding integrity in all circumstances. Help me to remain steadfast in Your truth, even when faced with pressure and temptation. May my life bring glory to Your name as I serve with integrity. Amen.

DAY 147

THE CALL OF DUTY: ANSWERING WITH FAITH

Scripture: "And I heard the voice of the Lord saying, 'Whom shall I send, and who will go for us?' Then I said, 'Here I am! Send me.'" - Isaiah 6:8 (ESV)

Just as Isaiah responded to God's call with faith and obedience, so too must you answer the call of duty with unwavering faith. Isaiah 6:8 reminds you of the privilege and responsibility of serving God's kingdom. When God calls you to a task, trust in His provision and guidance. Step out in faith, knowing that He equips and empowers you for every assignment. Let your life be a testimony of faithfulness and obedience to God's call.

Prayer: Sovereign Lord, as I answer Your call of duty, grant me the faith and courage to step out in obedience. Equip me for the tasks You have prepared for me, and guide me by Your Spirit. May I serve You faithfully and bring honor to Your name. Amen.

DAY 148

SPIRITUAL CAMOUFLAGE: BLENDING FAITH IN EVERYDAY LIFE

Scripture: "But be ye doers of the word, and not hearers only, deceiving your own selves." - James 1:22 (KJV)

In the hustle and bustle of everyday life, let your faith be evident through your actions. James 1:22 admonishes you to be doers of the Word, not just hearers, lest you deceive yourselves. Your life is a testimony of your faith, visible to all who observe you. Like a soldier blending into their surroundings with camouflage, let your faith permeate every aspect of your life, from your words and deeds to your attitudes and choices.

Prayer: Heavenly Father, help me to live out my faith in practical ways each day. May my life reflect Your love, grace, and truth to those around me. Empower me to be a doer of Your Word, living with integrity and authenticity in all I do. Amen.

DAY 149
COMMANDING CALM: MASTERING SELF-CONTROL IN TURBULENT TIMES

Scripture: "He that is slow to anger is better than the mighty; and he that ruleth his spirit than he that taketh a city." - Proverbs 16:32 (KJV)

In moments of turbulence and chaos, exercise self-control and command calm. Proverbs 16:32 teaches that one who rules their spirit is mightier than a conqueror. Just as Jesus calmed the storm with a word, so too can you cultivate inner peace and tranquility amidst life's storms. Through prayer, meditation, and reliance on God's Spirit, master your emotions and respond with grace and wisdom.

Prayer: Lord of peace, grant me the strength to master my emotions and command calm in turbulent times. Help me to rely on Your Spirit to guide my thoughts, words, and actions. May Your peace rule in my heart, even amidst life's storms. Amen.

DAY 150
DIVINE STRATEGY: APPLYING BIBLICAL WISDOM TO TACTICAL DECISIONS

Scripture: "For the Lord giveth wisdom: out of his mouth cometh knowledge and understanding." - Proverbs 2:6 (KJV)

As you make tactical decisions in life, seek divine strategy through biblical wisdom. Proverbs 2:6 assures that wisdom comes from the Lord, providing knowledge and understanding for every situation. Just as Joshua sought God's guidance before battle, so too can you seek His wisdom in your decision-making process. Through prayer and meditation on Scripture, align your strategies with God's purposes, trusting in His guidance and provision.

Prayer: Heavenly Father, grant me Your wisdom as I make tactical decisions in life. May Your Word be a lamp unto my feet and a light unto my path, guiding me in the way of righteousness. Help me to trust in Your providence and follow Your leading in all I do. Amen.

DAY 151
VALOR IN VULNERABILITY: EMBRACING EMOTIONAL STRENGTH

Scripture: "He healeth the broken in heart, and bindeth up their wounds." - Psalm 147:3 (KJV)

In a world that often values stoicism, Psalm 147:3 reminds you that there is valor in vulnerability. God doesn't expect you to suppress your emotions but invites you to bring them to Him for healing and restoration. Just as Jesus wept at the tomb of Lazarus, your emotions are not a sign of weakness but a reflection of your humanity. Embrace your emotional strength by acknowledging your feelings and bringing them to God in prayer.

Prayer: Gracious Father, thank You for being the healer of the broken-hearted. Help me to embrace my emotional strength and vulnerability, knowing that You are the source of my comfort and healing. Give me the courage to bring my emotions to You and trust in Your unfailing love. Amen.

DAY 152
GUIDED BY GRACE: NAVIGATING LIFE'S BATTLES WITH COMPASSION

Scripture: "Let us therefore come boldly unto the throne of grace, that we may obtain mercy, and find grace to help in time of need." - Hebrews 4:16 (KJV)

As you navigate life's battles, Hebrews 4:16 invites you to approach God's throne of grace with confidence, knowing that He offers mercy and compassion in abundance. Just as Jesus showed compassion to the woman caught in adultery and the lepers, so too can you extend grace and compassion to others in their time of need. Let your actions be guided by the love and compassion that flow from God's grace.

Prayer: Merciful Father, thank You for Your abundant grace and compassion. Guide me to navigate life's battles with the same love and mercy that You have shown me. Help me to extend grace to others, reflecting Your heart of compassion to the world. Amen.

DAY 153
UNSEEN WOUNDS: ADDRESSING THE SPIRITUAL IMPACT OF COMBAT

Scripture: "He healeth the broken in heart, and bindeth up their wounds." - Psalm 147:3 (KJV)

Just as physical wounds are evident in combat, there are unseen wounds that affect the spirit. Psalm 147:3 assures you that God is the healer of the broken hearted, addressing the spiritual impact of combat. Whether it's dealing with trauma, guilt, or loss, bring your unseen wounds to God for healing and restoration. His love and presence have the power to bring comfort and peace to the deepest recesses of your soul.

Prayer: Compassionate God, You see the unseen wounds that affect my spirit. Heal me, I pray, from the spiritual impact of combat. Bring comfort to my soul and peace to my troubled heart. May Your presence be a balm to my wounds, restoring me to wholeness. Amen.

DAY 154
STEADFAST IN SERVICE: CULTIVATING PATIENCE AND PERSEVERANCE

Scripture: "And let us not be weary in well doing: for in due season we shall reap, if we faint not." - Galatians 6:9 (KJV)

In the midst of challenges, Galatians 6:9 encourages you to remain steadfast in service, knowing that your labor is not in vain. Just as the Israelites persevered through the wilderness and the apostles endured persecution, so too can you cultivate patience and perseverance in your service. Trust in God's timing and His promise of a harvest for your faithful labor.

Prayer: Faithful God, grant me the patience and perseverance to remain steadfast in service. Help me to trust in Your timing and to continue doing good even when faced with challenges. May I reap a bountiful harvest as I faithfully serve You and others. Amen.

DAY 155
THE LIGHT OF LEADERSHIP: ILLUMINATING THE PATH FOR OTHERS

Scripture: "Let your light so shine before men, that they may see your good works, and glorify your Father which is in heaven." - Matthew 5:16 (KJV)

As a leader, Matthew 5:16 calls you to be a light in the darkness, illuminating the path for others to follow. Just as Jesus provided guidance and direction to His disciples, so too can you lead with integrity, wisdom, and compassion. Let your actions reflect the light of Christ, inspiring others to walk in His ways and glorify God.

Prayer: Heavenly Father, thank You for entrusting me with the responsibility of leadership. Help me to shine Your light brightly in the darkness, illuminating the path for others to follow. May my leadership bring glory to Your name and draw others closer to You. Amen.

DAY 156

SACRED DUTY: BALANCING MILITARY AND SPIRITUAL CALLINGS

Scripture: "But seek ye first the kingdom of God, and his righteousness; and all these things shall be added unto you." - Matthew 6:33 (KJV)

In the midst of your military duties, Matthew 6:33 reminds you to prioritize your spiritual calling and seek God's kingdom above all else. Just as Jesus balanced His earthly ministry with times of prayer and communion with the Father, so too can you integrate your military service with your spiritual walk. Trust in God to provide wisdom and guidance as you fulfill both your military and spiritual callings.

Prayer: Gracious God, help me to balance my military duties with my spiritual calling. May I seek Your kingdom first in all that I do, trusting You to provide for my needs and guide me in the path of righteousness. Give me wisdom to fulfill my sacred duty with honor and integrity. Amen.

DAY 157

THE HEART OF A WARRIOR: CULTIVATING LOVE AND KINDNESS IN THE FIELD

Scripture: "But the fruit of the Spirit is love, joy, peace, longsuffering, gentleness, goodness, faith, meekness, temperance: against such there is no law." - Galatians 5:22-23 (KJV)

As a warrior, Galatians 5:22-23 calls you to cultivate the fruit of the Spirit, including love, kindness, and gentleness, even in the midst of conflict. Just as Jesus demonstrated love and compassion to the Samaritan woman and the woman caught in adultery, so too can you show kindness and grace to those you encounter in the field. Let the love of Christ flow through you, touching the hearts of those around you.

Prayer: Loving Father, help me to cultivate the fruit of the Spirit in my heart, especially in the midst of conflict. May Your love and kindness overflow from me, touching the lives of those I encounter in the field. Use me as an instrument of Your peace and grace, bringing hope and healing to others. Amen.

DAY 158
DIVINE ORDERS: UNDERSTANDING YOUR SPIRITUAL MISSION

Scripture: "For I know the thoughts that I think toward you, saith the Lord, thoughts of peace, and not of evil, to give you an expected end." - Jeremiah 29:11 (KJV)

Jeremiah 29:11 assures you that God has a plan and purpose for your life, including your spiritual mission. Just as God called Moses to lead the Israelites out of Egypt and Paul to preach the Gospel to the Gentiles, so too has He ordained a divine mission for you. Seek His guidance and direction in understanding and fulfilling your spiritual calling.

Prayer: Sovereign God, thank You for the assurance that You have a plan and purpose for my life. Help me to understand and embrace the spiritual mission You have ordained for me. Give me clarity and courage to fulfil Your calling with faithfulness and obedience. Amen.

DAY 159
TACTICAL FAITH: DEPLOYING HOPE IN DIFFICULT MISSIONS

Scripture: "Now faith is the substance of things hoped for, the evidence of things not seen." - Hebrews 11:1 (KJV)

In the face of difficult missions, Hebrews 11:1 reminds you that faith is the substance of things hoped for, the evidence of things not seen. Just as Joshua trusted in God's promise of victory at Jericho and David relied on God's strength to defeat Goliath, so too can you deploy hope and faith in the most challenging circumstances. Let your trust in God be the foundation of your courage and confidence as you face difficult missions.

Prayer: Faithful God, strengthen my faith as I face difficult missions and challenges. Help me to deploy hope in the midst of uncertainty, knowing that You are faithful to fulfill Your promises. May my trust in You be unwavering, and my courage unshakeable, as I walk by faith and not by sight. Amen.

DAY 160
THE QUIET FRONT: FINDING SOLITUDE WITH GOD

Scripture: "Be still, and know that I am God: I will be exalted among the heathen, I will be exalted in the earth." - Psalm 46:10 (KJV)

In the midst of the chaos of life, Psalm 46:10 calls you to find solitude with God, knowing that He is sovereign and in control. Just as Jesus withdrew to lonely places to pray and commune with the Father, so too can you find solace and strength in the quiet presence of God. Set aside time each day to be still before Him, listening for His voice and seeking His guidance.

Prayer: Almighty God, teach me to find solitude with You in the midst of life's chaos. Help me to be still before You, knowing that You are sovereign and in control of all things. May my quiet times with You be a source of peace and strength, sustaining me in the midst of the storms of life. Amen.

DAY 161
COURAGEOUS COMPASSION: SERVING WITH EMPATHY

Scripture: "Finally, be ye all of one mind, having compassion one of another, love as brethren, be pitiful, be courteous." - 1 Peter 3:8 (KJV)

In 1 Peter 3:8, you're reminded to serve with courageous compassion, mirroring the love and empathy of Christ Himself. Just as Jesus showed compassion to the sick, the outcast, and the broken-hearted, you're called to extend empathy to those you encounter in your service. Let your actions be motivated by love, and let your heart be open to the needs of others.

Prayer: Gracious God, thank You for the example of Jesus, who showed us how to serve with courageous compassion. Fill my heart with empathy and love, that I may reflect Your compassion to those in need. Help me to serve others with kindness and humility, following the example of Your Son. Amen.

DAY 162

THE WARRIOR'S REST: EMBRACING GOD'S PEACE IN DOWNTIME

Scripture: "Come unto me, all ye that labour and are heavy laden, and I will give you rest." - Matthew 11:28 (KJV)

In Matthew 11:28, Jesus invites you to find rest in Him, especially during times of downtime. Just as Jesus sought moments of solitude to pray and recharge, you're encouraged to embrace God's peace and rest in His presence. Use your downtime to seek Him, to find refreshment for your soul, and to be rejuvenated for the battles ahead.

Prayer: Loving Father, thank You for the promise of rest that we find in Your Son, Jesus Christ. Help me to embrace Your peace during times of downtime, that I may find rest for my soul in Your presence. Renew me, Lord, and empower me to continue serving You faithfully. Amen.

DAY 163
TACTICAL PRAYERS: SEEKING GUIDANCE FOR STRATEGIC DECISIONS

Scripture: "If any of you lack wisdom, let him ask of God, that giveth to all men liberally, and upbraideth not; and it shall be given him." - James 1:5 (KJV)

James 1:5 reminds you that God is the source of wisdom, and He invites you to seek His guidance through prayer, especially when facing strategic decisions. Just as King Solomon sought wisdom from God when ruling over Israel, so too can you seek divine guidance for the decisions you must make. Approach God with humility and faith, trusting that He will provide the wisdom you need.

Prayer: Heavenly Father, I come to You seeking wisdom for the strategic decisions I must make. Grant me discernment, Lord, that I may make choices that align with Your will and bring glory to Your name. Guide me, Holy Spirit, and lead me in the paths of righteousness. Amen.

DAY 164
THE VALOR OF FORGIVENESS: HEALING FROM THE HARDSHIPS OF DUTY

Scripture: "And be ye kind one to another, tender-hearted, forgiving one another, even as God for Christ's sake hath forgiven you." - Ephesians 4:32 (KJV)

In Ephesians 4:32, you're reminded of the importance of forgiveness in healing from the hardships of duty. Just as God has forgiven you through the sacrifice of Christ, so too are you called to extend forgiveness to others. Release the burdens of resentment and bitterness, and let the healing power of forgiveness bring restoration to your soul.

Prayer: Gracious God, thank You for the gift of forgiveness that You have given us through Your Son, Jesus Christ. Help me to extend that same forgiveness to others, especially in the midst of the hardships of duty. Heal my heart, Lord, and fill me with Your peace and grace. Amen.

DAY 165

SPIRITUAL RECONNAISSANCE:

UNDERSTANDING GOD'S VISION FOR YOUR LIFE

Scripture: "For I know the thoughts that I think toward you, saith the Lord, thoughts of peace, and not of evil, to give you an expected end." - Jeremiah 29:11 (KJV)

Jeremiah 29:11 assures you that God has a plan and a vision for your life, one filled with hope and purpose. Just as God called Jeremiah to be a prophet to the nations, so too does He have a unique purpose and plan for your life. Take time in prayer and reflection to seek God's vision for your life, trusting that He will reveal His plans to you in His perfect timing.

Prayer: Sovereign God, thank You for the assurance that You have a plan and a purpose for my life. Open my eyes, Lord, to see Your vision for me, and give me the courage to walk in obedience to Your will. May Your plans for me be fulfilled, and may Your name be glorified in my life. Amen.

DAY 166

DIVINE DEPLOYMENT: TRUSTING GOD'S PLAN IN UNCERTAIN TIMES

Scripture: "Trust in the Lord with all thine heart; and lean not unto thine own understanding. In all thy ways acknowledge him, and he shall direct thy paths." - Proverbs 3:5-6 (KJV)

Proverbs 3:5-6 reminds you to trust in the Lord's plan, even in times of uncertainty. Just as God led the Israelites through the wilderness with a pillar of cloud by day and a pillar of fire by night, so too will He guide you through the uncertainties of life. Trust in His wisdom and sovereignty, knowing that He holds your future in His hands.

Prayer: Faithful God, I surrender my plans and my future into Your hands. Help me to trust in Your divine deployment, even in times of uncertainty. Guide me, Lord, and direct my paths according to Your will. May Your peace reign in my heart, knowing that You are in control. Amen.

DAY 167

THE FELLOWSHIP OF THE FAITHFUL: BUILDING BONDS BEYOND BATTLE

Scripture: "And let us consider one another to provoke unto love and to good works: Not forsaking the assembling of ourselves together, as the manner of some is; but exhorting one another: and so much the more, as ye see the day approaching." - Hebrews 10:24-25 (KJV)

Hebrews 10:24-25 encourages you to build bonds of fellowship with other believers, especially in times of trial and battle. Just as Paul urged the early Christians to encourage and exhort one another, so too can you find strength and support in the fellowship of the faithful. Reach out to your brothers and sisters in Christ, sharing burdens and lifting each other up in prayer and encouragement.

Prayer: Gracious Father, thank You for the fellowship of the faithful, where we can find strength and support in times of trial. Help us to build deep bonds of love and friendship with one another, that we may encourage and exhort one another in our faith. Bless our fellowship, Lord, and use it to glorify Your name. Amen.

DAY 168
HONORING THE SACRIFICE: SPIRITUAL REFLECTIONS ON SERVICE

Scripture: "Greater love hath no man than this, that a man lay down his life for his friends." - John 15:13 (KJV)

In John 15:13, Jesus speaks of the ultimate sacrifice of laying down one's life for others, a sacrifice that embodies true love and honor. Just as Jesus willingly laid down His life for the salvation of mankind, so too do you honor His sacrifice through your service to others. Take time to reflect on the spiritual significance of your service, knowing that every act of sacrifice and selflessness brings glory to God.

Prayer: Gracious God, thank You for the example of Jesus, who laid down His life for us out of love. Help me to honor His sacrifice through my service to others, whether in times of peace or in times of conflict. May my life be a living sacrifice, pleasing and acceptable in Your sight. Amen.

DAY 169
THE DISCIPLINE OF HOPE: MAINTAINING POSITIVITY IN ADVERSITY

Scripture: "Now the God of hope fill you with all joy and peace in believing, that ye may abound in hope, through the power of the Holy Ghost." - Romans 15:13 (KJV)

Romans 15:13 encourages you to maintain hope and positivity, even in the face of adversity. Just as Paul prayed for the believers in Rome to abound in hope through the power of the Holy Spirit, so too can you cultivate a spirit of hopefulness in every circumstance. Trust in God's promises, knowing that He is faithful to fulfill them, and let the hope of His presence fill you with joy and peace.

Prayer: Heavenly Father, fill me with the hope, joy, and peace that come from believing in You. Help me to maintain positivity in the midst of adversity, trusting in Your promises and Your presence. May the power of the Holy Spirit work in me to abound in hope, even in the darkest of times. Amen.

DAY 170
SPIRITUAL WARFARE: BATTLING TEMPTATION WITH FAITH

Scripture: "Submit yourselves therefore to God. Resist the devil, and he will flee from you." - James 4:7 (KJV)

In James 4:7, you're reminded of the spiritual battle against temptation, and the importance of standing firm in faith. Just as Jesus resisted the devil's temptations in the wilderness by quoting Scripture, so too can you overcome temptation by submitting to God and resisting the enemy. Arm yourself with the Word of God, and rely on the power of the Holy Spirit to help you stand strong in faith.

Prayer: Almighty God, I submit myself to You, knowing that You alone have the power to overcome temptation. Strengthen me, Lord, to resist the schemes of the enemy, and help me to stand firm in faith. Grant me discernment to recognize temptation, and courage to overcome it through Your Word and Your Spirit. May Your victory be proclaimed in my life, to Your glory. Amen.

DAY 171

THE SENTINEL'S PRAYER: WATCHING OVER COMRADES WITH FAITH

Scripture: "Watch ye, stand fast in the faith, quit you like men, be strong." - 1 Corinthians 16:13 (KJV)

In 1 Corinthians 16:13, Paul urges believers to be vigilant, standing firm in faith and strength. As a sentinel, your prayerful watch over your comrades reflects this vigilant faith. Just as a sentinel keeps watch over the camp, so too do you watch over your fellow soldiers in prayer. Your intercession acts as a shield, protecting them from spiritual harm and strengthening them for the battles ahead.

Prayer: Gracious God, as I stand watch over my comrades, I lift them up to You in prayer. Grant them strength and courage for the challenges they face. Protect them from harm, both seen and unseen, and surround them with Your presence. Help me to be faithful in my duty as a sentinel, watching over them with love and faith. Amen.

DAY 172

DIVINE DRILL: SPIRITUAL EXERCISES FOR THE DISCIPLINED SOUL

Scripture: "But strong meat belongeth to them that are of full age, even those who by reason of use have their senses exercised to discern both good and evil." - Hebrews 5:14 (KJV)

Hebrews 5:14 speaks of the importance of spiritual exercise, which strengthens the soul and sharpens discernment. Just as physical exercise strengthens the body, so too do spiritual exercises strengthen the soul. Through prayer, meditation, Scripture study, and fellowship, you discipline your soul, training it to discern between good and evil.

Prayer: Heavenly Father, thank You for the spiritual exercises that strengthen my soul. Help me to be disciplined in prayer, diligent in studying Your Word, and faithful in fellowship with other believers. May my senses be exercised to discern both good and evil, that I may walk in Your ways. Amen.

DAY 173
THE SHIELD OF BELIEF: DEFENDING AGAINST SPIRITUAL ADVERSITY

Scripture: "Above all, taking the shield of faith, wherewith ye shall be able to quench all the fiery darts of the wicked." - Ephesians 6:16 (KJV)

Ephesians 6:16 describes faith as a shield that protects against the attacks of the enemy. Just as a shield deflects arrows and spears in battle, so too does faith deflect the fiery darts of doubt, fear, and temptation. By trusting in God's promises and believing in His power, you can withstand any assault on your faith.

Prayer: Gracious God, I take up the shield of faith to defend against spiritual adversity. Strengthen my belief in Your promises, Lord, and help me to trust in Your unfailing love and protection. May my faith be a shield that quenches every fiery dart of the enemy. Amen.

DAY 174
CAMARADERIE IN CHRIST: STRENGTHENING BONDS THROUGH SHARED FAITH

Scripture: "And they continued stedfastly in the apostles' doctrine and fellowship, and in breaking of bread, and in prayers." - Acts 2:42 (KJV)

Acts 2:42 highlights the importance of fellowship among believers, as they shared in the apostles' teaching, fellowship, and prayer. Just as the early Christians strengthened their bonds through shared faith and fellowship, so too can you find camaraderie in Christ. By coming together with fellow believers, you can encourage one another, share burdens, and lift each other up in prayer.

Prayer: Loving Father, thank You for the gift of fellowship with other believers. Help us to strengthen our bonds through shared faith and prayer. May our camaraderie in Christ be a source of encouragement and support, as we journey together in faith. Amen.

DAY 175
STRATEGIC PATIENCE: WAITING ON GOD'S TIMING IN WARFARE

Scripture: "Rest in the Lord, and wait patiently for him: fret not thyself because of him who prospereth in his way, because of the man who bringeth wicked devices to pass." - Psalm 37:7 (KJV)

Psalm 37:7 encourages you to wait patiently on the Lord, trusting in His timing and His ways. Just as a soldier must wait for the right moment to execute a strategic maneuver, so too must you wait on God's timing in the battles of life. Trust that His plans are perfect, and His timing is impeccable, even when circumstances seem dire.

Prayer: Heavenly Father, teach me to wait patiently on You, trusting in Your perfect timing. Help me to rest in Your promises, even when the enemy prospers. Grant me the wisdom to discern Your will and the patience to wait for Your direction. Amen.

DAY 176
THE GENERAL'S WISDOM: APPLYING SCRIPTURAL STRATEGY TO LIFE'S BATTLES

Scripture: "Wisdom is the principal thing; therefore get wisdom: and with all thy getting get understanding." - Proverbs 4:7 (KJV)

Proverbs 4:7 emphasizes the importance of wisdom in navigating life's battles, both spiritual and physical. Just as a general must devise strategic plans to achieve victory on the battlefield, so too must you seek God's wisdom to overcome the challenges you face. By applying Scriptural principles to your life, you gain understanding and insight to make wise decisions.

Prayer: Gracious God, grant me Your wisdom to navigate life's battles. Help me to apply Your Word to every situation, that I may gain understanding and insight. May Your wisdom guide my steps and lead me to victory in Christ. Amen.

DAY 177
SPIRITUAL BOOT CAMP: BUILDING ENDURANCE FOR THE SOUL

Scripture: "And not only so, but we glory in tribulations also: knowing that tribulation worketh patience; And patience, experience; and experience, hope." - Romans 5:3-4 (KJV)

Romans 5:3-4 reminds you that trials build endurance, which leads to hope. Just as boot camp strengthens a soldier's physical endurance, so too does spiritual adversity build endurance for the soul. By persevering through trials, you develop spiritual resilience and deepen your reliance on God.

Prayer: Heavenly Father, thank You for the spiritual boot camp that builds endurance for my soul. Help me to embrace trials as opportunities for growth, knowing that they produce perseverance, character, and hope. Strengthen me, Lord, that I may endure every challenge with faith and courage. Amen.

DAY 178

THE PEACEKEEPER'S PROMISE: UPHOLDING SERENITY AMIDST STRIFE

Scripture: "Thou wilt keep him in perfect peace, whose mind is stayed on thee: because he trusteth in thee." - Isaiah 26:3 (KJV)

Isaiah 26:3 assures you that God will keep you in perfect peace when you trust in Him. Just as a peacekeeper maintains calm in the midst of conflict, so too can you uphold serenity by fixing your thoughts on God and trusting in His promises. In the chaos of life's battles, God offers peace that surpasses understanding.

Prayer: Gracious God, thank You for the promise of perfect peace when we trust in You. Keep our minds steadfast on You, Lord, that we may experience Your peace amidst life's storms. Help us to be peacemakers in a world filled with strife, reflecting Your love and grace. Amen.

DAY 179
MISSION BRIEFING: ALIGNING DAILY DUTIES
WITH DIVINE PURPOSE

Scripture: "Commit thy works unto the Lord, and thy thoughts shall be established." - Proverbs 16:3 (KJV)

Proverbs 16:3 encourages you to commit your plans to the Lord, trusting Him to establish them. Just as a soldier receives a mission briefing to align their actions with the overall objective, so too must you commit your works to the Lord, seeking His guidance and direction in all you do. By aligning your daily duties with God's divine purpose, you walk in His will and experience His blessing.

Prayer: Heavenly Father, as I embark on each day's mission, I commit my works to You. Guide me, Lord, in aligning my actions with Your divine purpose, that Your will may be accomplished in my life. May my thoughts and deeds bring glory to Your name. Amen.

DAY 180
THE WARRIOR'S WORSHIP: OFFERING PRAISE
IN THE MIDST OF DUTY

Scripture: "O come, let us worship and bow down: let us kneel before the Lord our maker." - Psalm 95:6 (KJV)

Psalm 95:6 calls you to worship the Lord, acknowledging Him as your Maker and King. Just as a warrior pauses to worship amidst the demands of duty, so too must you offer praise to God in the midst of life's battles. Worship is a powerful weapon against the enemy, reminding you of God's sovereignty and strengthening your faith.

Prayer: Gracious God, I worship You as my Maker and King. In the midst of life's battles, may my heart overflow with praise and adoration for You. Help me to worship You in spirit and in truth, knowing that You are worthy of all honor and glory. Amen.

DAY 181
THE WARRIOR'S PATH: WALKING IN RIGHTEOUSNESS

Scripture: "He restoreth my soul: he leadeth me in the paths of righteousness for his name's sake." - Psalm 23:3 (KJV)

Psalm 23:3 illustrates God's role in leading His people along the paths of righteousness. Just as a shepherd guides his sheep along safe and righteous paths, so too does God lead His warriors along the path of righteousness for His glory. As a warrior in God's army, you are called to walk in righteousness, following the example set by Jesus Christ. Your conduct, decisions, and interactions should reflect God's righteousness, shining as a beacon of light in a world filled with darkness.

Prayer: Heavenly Father, lead me along the path of righteousness for Your name's sake. Help me to walk in obedience to Your Word and to follow the example of Jesus Christ in all things. May my life bring glory to Your name as I strive to live in righteousness each day. Amen.

DAY 182
SPIRITUAL TACTICS: OVERCOMING LIFE'S OBSTACLES WITH FAITH

Scripture: "For whatsoever is born of God overcometh the world: and this is the victory that overcometh the world, even our faith." - 1 John 5:4 (KJV)

1 John 5:4 reminds us that our faith in God enables us to overcome the obstacles of this world. Just as a skilled tactician devises strategies to overcome enemy obstacles, so too does our faith enable us to overcome life's challenges. In the face of adversity, trust in God's promises and lean on His strength. By deploying the spiritual tactics of prayer, Scripture study, and fellowship, you can navigate life's obstacles with confidence and resilience.

Prayer: Gracious God, grant me the wisdom to overcome life's obstacles with faith. Strengthen me, Lord, to trust in Your promises and to rely on Your strength in every situation. Guide me in deploying spiritual tactics to navigate life's challenges with confidence and resilience. Amen.

DAY 183

THE FAITHFUL LEADER: GUIDING WITH GOD'S WISDOM

Scripture: "If any of you lack wisdom, let him ask of God, that giveth to all men liberally, and upbraideth not; and it shall be given him." - James 1:5 (KJV)

James 1:5 assures us that God generously gives wisdom to those who ask. As a faithful leader, seek God's wisdom to guide those under your care. Just as a skilled leader relies on intelligence and insight to make informed decisions, so too does a faithful leader rely on God's wisdom. By seeking His guidance through prayer and Scripture, you can lead with integrity and discernment.

Prayer: Heavenly Father, grant me Your wisdom as I lead others in Your name. Help me to seek Your guidance in all decisions, that I may lead with integrity and discernment. May Your wisdom guide my words and actions, bringing glory to Your name. Amen.

DAY 184

DIVINE ENDURANCE: RUNNING THE RACE WITH PERSEVERANCE

Scripture: "Wherefore seeing we also are compassed about with so great a cloud of witnesses, let us lay aside every weight, and the sin which doth so easily beset us, and let us run with patience the race that is set before us." - Hebrews 12:1 (KJV)

Hebrews 12:1 encourages us to run the race of faith with patience, laying aside anything that hinders us. Like a marathon runner, endure with perseverance, keeping your eyes fixed on Jesus. Just as a runner endures physical strain to reach the finish line, so too must you endure spiritual challenges to fulfill God's purpose for your life. Lean on His strength and trust in His promises, knowing that He will sustain you through every trial.

Prayer: Gracious God, grant me divine endurance to run the race of faith with perseverance. Help me to lay aside every weight and sin that hinders me, fixing my eyes on Jesus, the author and finisher of my faith. Strengthen me, Lord, to endure every trial and to finish the race well. Amen.

DAY 185
THE PRAYER BATTALION: UNITING IN INTERCESSION FOR COMRADES

Scripture: "Confess your faults one to another, and pray one for another, that ye may be healed. The effectual fervent prayer of a righteous man availeth much." - James 5:16 (KJV)

James 5:16 emphasizes the power of united prayer among believers. Just as soldiers rally together in battle, so too should believers unite in intercessory prayer for one another's needs. As part of the prayer battalion, lift up your comrades in prayer, interceding for their needs, protection, and spiritual growth. Through fervent and effectual prayer, you can make a significant impact on the lives of others.

Prayer: Heavenly Father, unite us as a prayer battalion, interceding for one another with fervent hearts. Help us to lift up our comrades in prayer, seeking Your provision, protection, and healing in their lives. May our prayers avail much for Your glory and the advancement of Your kingdom. Amen.

DAY 186
SPIRITUAL MEDALS OF HONOR: RECOGNIZING ACTS OF FAITH

Scripture: "And let us not be weary in well doing: for in due season we shall reap, if we faint not." - Galatians 6:9 (KJV)

Galatians 6:9 encourages us not to grow weary in doing good, for our acts of faith will be rewarded. Just as soldiers are honored with medals for acts of valor, so too will God recognize and reward acts of faith. As you faithfully serve God and others, know that every act of kindness, sacrifice, and obedience is seen and valued by God. Even in moments when it feels challenging, persevere in doing good, trusting that God will reward your faithfulness in due time.

Prayer: Gracious God, thank You for recognizing and rewarding acts of faith. Help us to persevere in doing good, knowing that our labor in Your name is not in vain. Strengthen us, Lord, to continue serving faithfully, trusting in Your promise of reward. Amen.

DAY 187
THE SPIRITUAL SENTINEL: STANDING GUARD OVER YOUR HEART AND MIND

Scripture: "Keep thy heart with all diligence; for out of it are the issues of life." - Proverbs 4:23 (KJV)

Proverbs 4:23 admonishes us to guard our hearts diligently, for they determine the course of our lives. Just as a sentinel stands guard to protect against threats, so too must we protect our hearts and minds from spiritual danger. As a spiritual sentinel, be vigilant in guarding your heart against negative influences, sinful desires, and harmful thoughts. Fill your mind with God's Word, prayer, and worship, standing firm against the enemy's attacks.

Prayer: Heavenly Father, help us to be vigilant spiritual sentinels, guarding our hearts and minds with diligence. Protect us from the schemes of the enemy and strengthen us to resist temptation. May our hearts be filled with Your truth and our minds renewed by Your Spirit. Amen.

DAY 188
THE SOLDIER'S CREED: LIVING A LIFE OF SPIRITUAL DISCIPLINE

Scripture: "And he said to them all, If any man will come after me, let him deny himself, and take up his cross daily, and follow me." - Luke 9:23 (KJV)

Luke 9:23 outlines the soldier's creed of following Jesus, which requires self-denial, daily cross-bearing, and unwavering commitment. Just as soldiers adhere to a code of discipline, so too must believers live lives of spiritual discipline. As you follow Jesus, embrace the disciplines of prayer, Scripture study, fasting, and obedience. These disciplines cultivate spiritual maturity, strengthen your faith, and deepen your relationship with God.

Prayer: Gracious God, help us to live according to the soldier's creed of following Jesus. Grant us the discipline to deny ourselves, take up our crosses daily, and follow You wholeheartedly. May our lives reflect the commitment and obedience of true disciples. Amen.

DAY 189
BATTLEFIELD BLESSINGS: FINDING GOD'S PRESENCE IN HARDSHIP

Scripture: "The Lord is my shepherd; I shall not want. He maketh me to lie down in green pastures: he leadeth me beside the still waters." - Psalm 23:1-2 (KJV)

Psalm 23:1-2 assures us of God's provision and presence, even in the midst of hardship. Just as a shepherd cares for his flock in the midst of danger, so too does God comfort and sustain us in times of trial. In the battlefield of life, trust in God's presence and provision, knowing that He is with you always. Even in the midst of hardship, He provides green pastures of rest and still waters of peace for your soul.

Prayer: Heavenly Father, thank You for Your presence and provision in the midst of life's battles. Help us to trust in Your care and to find comfort in Your presence, even in times of hardship. May Your peace sustain us and Your presence guide us through every trial. Amen.

DAY 190
THE STRATEGY ROOM: PLANNING WITH PURPOSE AND PRAYER

Scripture: "Commit thy works unto the Lord, and thy thoughts shall be established." - Proverbs 16:3 (KJV)

Proverbs 16:3 encourages us to commit our plans to the Lord, trusting Him to establish them. Just as military leaders strategize for victory, so too must we plan with purpose and prayer, seeking God's guidance in all we do.

Before entering the battlefield of each day, seek God's wisdom and direction for your plans and decisions. By aligning your strategies with His purposes, you can navigate life's challenges with confidence and effectiveness.

Prayer: Gracious God, as we enter the strategy room of planning, we commit our works to You. Guide us, Lord, in aligning our plans with Your purposes, that Your will may be accomplished in our lives. Grant us wisdom and discernment as we seek Your guidance in all we do. Amen.

DAY 191
SPIRITUAL FORTIFICATIONS: BUILDING DEFENSES WITH FAITH AND PRAYER

Scripture: "Finally, my brethren, be strong in the Lord, and in the power of his might. Put on the whole armour of God, that ye may be able to stand against the wiles of the devil." - Ephesians 6:10-11 (KJV)

Ephesians 6:10-11 reminds us of the spiritual battle we face and the necessity of fortifying ourselves with God's armor. Just as a fortress is built to withstand attacks, so too must we fortify ourselves with faith and prayer to resist the schemes of the enemy. As you face spiritual battles, clothe yourself with the armor of God: truth, righteousness, the gospel of peace, faith, salvation, and the Word of God. By fortifying yourself with these spiritual defenses, you can stand firm against the enemy's attacks.

Prayer: Heavenly Father, strengthen us with Your might as we build spiritual fortifications in our lives. Help us to put on the whole armor of God, that we may stand firm against the enemy's schemes. May our faith and prayer be our strong defenses in the battles we face. Amen.

DAY 192
THE WARRIOR'S REFLECTION: MEDITATING ON GOD'S PROMISES

Scripture: "This book of the law shall not depart out of thy mouth; but thou shalt meditate therein day and night, that thou mayest observe to do according to all that is written therein: for then thou shalt make thy way prosperous, and then thou shalt have good success." - Joshua 1:8 (KJV)

Joshua 1:8 highlights the importance of meditating on God's Word day and night. Just as a warrior reflects on battle strategies, so too must we meditate on God's promises to navigate life's challenges. As you meditate on God's Word, His promises will become the foundation of your faith and the guiding light for your path. Reflect on His faithfulness, His love, and His provision, finding strength and encouragement in His promises.

Prayer: Gracious God, help us to meditate on Your Word day and night, finding strength and guidance in Your promises. May Your Word be a lamp unto our feet and a light unto our path as we navigate life's challenges. Amen.

DAY 193
DIVINE LOGISTICS: ORGANIZING LIFE WITH GODLY PRIORITIES

Scripture: "But seek ye first the kingdom of God, and his righteousness; and all these things shall be added unto you." - Matthew 6:33 (KJV)

Matthew 6:33 encourages us to prioritize seeking God's kingdom and righteousness above all else. Just as a military commander organizes logistics for strategic advantage, so too must we organize our lives around Godly priorities. As you prioritize seeking God's kingdom and righteousness, align your goals, plans, and actions with His will. Seek His guidance in all you do, trusting that He will provide for your needs and bless your endeavors.

Prayer: Heavenly Father, help us to prioritize seeking Your kingdom and righteousness above all else. Guide us in organizing our lives around Your priorities, that we may walk in Your will and experience Your blessings. Amen.

DAY 194: THE FAITHFUL TROOPER: PERSEVERING IN PRAYER AND PURPOSE

Scripture: "And let us not be weary in well doing: for in due season we shall reap, if we faint not." - Galatians 6:9 (KJV)

Galatians 6:9 encourages us not to grow weary in doing good, for our perseverance will lead to a harvest of blessings. Just as a trooper remains steadfast in duty, so too must we persevere in prayer and purpose. As you face challenges and obstacles, continue to pray without ceasing, trusting in God's faithfulness and provision. Persevere in doing good, knowing that God sees your efforts and will reward your faithfulness in due time.

Prayer: Gracious God, strengthen us to persevere in prayer and purpose, even in the face of challenges and obstacles. Help us to remain steadfast in doing good, trusting in Your faithfulness and provision. May our perseverance lead to a harvest of blessings for Your glory. Amen.

DAY 195

THE CHAPLAIN'S MESSAGE: ENCOURAGEMENT FOR THE FRONT LINES

Scripture: "Let us hold fast the profession of our faith without wavering; (for he is faithful that promised;)" - Hebrews 10:23 (KJV)

Hebrews 10:23 encourages us to hold fast to our faith without wavering, for God is faithful to His promises. Just as a chaplain brings encouragement to the front lines, so too must we uplift and support one another in faith. As you face battles and trials, be a source of encouragement to those around you, reminding them of God's faithfulness and promises. Share His Word, offer prayers, and extend a helping hand, reflecting His love and compassion to others.

Prayer: Heavenly Father, use us as instruments of encouragement to those on the front lines of faith. Help us to hold fast to our profession of faith without wavering, trusting in Your faithfulness and promises. May Your love and compassion flow through us to uplift and support others. Amen.

DAY 196

SPIRITUAL RECON: SCOUTING AHEAD WITH HOPE AND TRUST

Scripture: "Trust in the Lord with all thine heart; and lean not unto thine own understanding. In all thy ways acknowledge him, and he shall direct thy paths." - Proverbs 3:5-6 (KJV)

Proverbs 3:5-6 urges us to trust in the Lord with all our hearts and lean not on our own understanding. Just as scouts venture ahead to gather intelligence, so too must we scout ahead in life with hope and trust in God's guidance. As you navigate life's uncertainties, trust in the Lord's wisdom and direction, acknowledging Him in all your ways. Step forward with confidence, knowing that He will lead and guide you according to His perfect plan.

Prayer: Gracious God, help us to trust in You with all our hearts and lean not on our own understanding. Guide us as we scout ahead in life, seeking Your wisdom and direction in all we do. May Your presence give us hope and assurance for the journey ahead. Amen.

DAY 197
THE SOLDIER'S HYMN: SINGING PRAISES IN THE MIDST OF BATTLE

Scripture: "I will bless the Lord at all times: his praise shall continually be in my mouth." - Psalm 34:1 (KJV)

Psalm 34:1 declares the intention to bless the Lord at all times and continually praise Him. Just as soldiers sing hymns of praise on the battlefield, so too must we lift our voices in worship amidst life's battles. As you face challenges and trials, let praise be on your lips, magnifying the Lord for His goodness and faithfulness. Sing hymns of praise, offer prayers of thanksgiving, and declare His glory, knowing that He is worthy of all praise.

Prayer: Heavenly Father, may our lives be a constant hymn of praise to Your name, regardless of the battles we face. Fill our hearts with gratitude and joy as we lift our voices in worship, declaring Your goodness and faithfulness. Amen.

DAY 198
NIGHT WATCH WHISPERS: PRAYERS UNDER THE STARS

Scripture: "But thou, when thou prayest, enter into thy closet, and when thou hast shut thy door, pray to thy Father which is in secret; and thy Father which seeth in secret shall reward thee openly." - Matthew 6:6 (KJV)

Matthew 6:6 encourages us to pray in secret, knowing that our Heavenly Father sees and rewards our prayers. Just as soldiers offer prayers under the stars during the night watch, so too must we commune with God in the quiet of our hearts. As you spend time in prayer, whether under the stars or in the privacy of your room, pour out your heart to God with honesty and sincerity. Trust that He hears your prayers and will answer them according to His perfect will.

Prayer: Gracious God, as we offer prayers under the stars and in the quiet of our hearts, hear our petitions and grant us Your peace. May our communion with You be sweet, and may Your presence fill us with hope and assurance. Amen.

DAY 199
THE COMPASS ROSE: NAVIGATING LIFE'S MORAL COORDINATES

Scripture: "Thy word is a lamp unto my feet, and a light unto my path." - Psalm 119:105 (KJV)

Psalm 119:105 describes God's Word as a lamp to guide our steps and a light to illuminate our path. Just as a compass rose provides direction, so too does God's Word guide us in navigating life's moral coordinates. As you face decisions and choices, consult God's Word for wisdom and direction. Let His truth be your moral compass, guiding you to walk in righteousness and integrity in all areas of life.

Prayer: Heavenly Father, thank You for Your Word, which serves as our guide in navigating life's moral coordinates. Grant us wisdom and discernment to walk in Your ways, following the path of righteousness and integrity. May Your Word be a lamp to our feet and a light to our path. Amen.

DAY 200
DAWN'S EARLY LIGHT: RENEWAL AND RESOLVE IN THE MORNING MARCH

Scripture: "But they that wait upon the Lord shall renew their strength; they shall mount up with wings as eagles; they shall run, and not be weary; and they shall walk, and not faint." - Isaiah 40:31 (KJV)

Isaiah 40:31 promises renewal and strength to those who wait upon the Lord. Just as soldiers march forward with renewed vigor at dawn's early light, so too must we find renewal and resolve in seeking God's presence each morning. As you begin each day, seek the Lord in prayer and meditation, allowing Him to renew your strength and fill you with His peace. Trust in His promises, knowing that He will guide you through the day's challenges with grace and wisdom.

Prayer: Gracious God, as we march forward into each new day, renew our strength and fill us with Your peace. May Your presence be our constant companion, guiding us with wisdom and grace. Grant us resolve to walk in Your ways and fulfill Your purposes. Amen.

DAY 201
FINDING PEACE AMIDST CHAOS: STRATEGIES FOR INNER CALM

Scripture: "Peace I leave with you, my peace I give unto you: not as the world giveth, give I unto you. Let not your heart be troubled, neither let it be afraid." - John 14:27 (KJV)

John 14:27 offers a profound promise of peace from Jesus Himself. In the midst of chaos and turmoil, His peace surpasses all understanding, providing a sanctuary for your soul. Amid life's storms, anchor yourself in prayer and meditation on God's Word. By surrendering your worries and fears to Him, you open your heart to receive His peace that transcends earthly troubles.

Prayer: Heavenly Father, in the midst of chaos, grant us Your peace that surpasses all understanding. Help us to anchor ourselves in You, finding calm amidst life's storms. May Your presence be our refuge and strength, sustaining us through every trial. Amen.

DAY 202
EMBRACING RESILIENCE IN THE FACE OF ADVERSITY

Scripture: "But he giveth more grace. Wherefore he saith, God resisteth the proud, but giveth grace unto the humble." - James 4:6 (KJV)

James 4:6 reminds us of God's promise to grant grace to the humble. In times of adversity, humility allows us to draw upon His strength and resilience to overcome. In the face of trials, embrace humility and rely on God's grace to sustain you. Through prayer, surrender your struggles to Him, trusting that He will provide the resilience needed to endure and overcome.

Prayer: Gracious God, grant us the humility to rely on Your grace in times of adversity. Strengthen us with resilience to face every challenge, knowing that Your power is made perfect in our weakness. May Your grace sustain us and lead us to victory. Amen.

DAY 203
TRUSTING IN DIVINE GUIDANCE DURING DIFFICULT TIMES

Scripture: "Trust in the Lord with all thine heart; and lean not unto thine own understanding. In all thy ways acknowledge him, and he shall direct thy paths." - Proverbs 3:5-6 (KJV)

Proverbs 3:5-6 implores us to trust in the Lord wholeheartedly and acknowledge Him in all our ways. In times of difficulty, trust in His guidance, knowing that He will direct your path. As you face uncertainty, surrender control to God and trust in His wisdom and sovereignty. Through prayer and seeking His Word, allow Him to illuminate your path and lead you through every trial.

Prayer: Heavenly Father, in times of difficulty, grant us the faith to trust in Your divine guidance. Help us to surrender control to You and acknowledge Your wisdom in all our ways. Lead us on the path of righteousness and peace, for Your glory. Amen.

DAY 204

CULTIVATING COURAGE IN UNCERTAIN CIRCUMSTANCES

Scripture: "Be strong and of a good courage, fear not, nor be afraid of them: for the Lord thy God, he it is that doth go with thee; he will not fail thee, nor forsake thee." - Deuteronomy 31:6 (KJV)

Deuteronomy 31:6 encourages us to be strong and courageous, knowing that the Lord goes with us and will never leave nor forsake us. In uncertain circumstances, draw upon His presence and promises for courage. As you face challenges, cling to God's faithfulness and presence. Through prayer and reliance on His Word, cultivate courage that surpasses worldly fears, knowing that He is with you every step of the way.

Prayer: Gracious God, grant us the courage to face uncertain circumstances with faith and confidence in Your promises. May Your presence be our strength and refuge, empowering us to overcome every obstacle. Help us to trust in Your unfailing love and provision. Amen.

DAY 205

NURTURING RELATIONSHIPS: BUILDING A SUPPORTIVE NETWORK

Scripture: "Two are better than one; because they have a good reward for their labour. For if they fall, the one will lift up his fellow: but woe to him that is alone when he falleth; for he hath not another to help him up." - Ecclesiastes 4:9-10 (KJV)

Ecclesiastes 4:9-10 emphasizes the importance of supportive relationships. In building a network of support, surround yourself with fellow believers who can uplift and encourage you in times of need. As you nurture relationships, prioritize authentic connections built on love, trust, and mutual support. Through prayer and fellowship, cultivate a supportive network that strengthens your faith and helps you navigate life's challenges.

Prayer: Heavenly Father, thank You for the gift of supportive relationships. Help us to nurture connections built on love, trust, and mutual support. May our relationships be a source of encouragement and strength as we journey together in faith. Amen.

DAY 206

OVERCOMING FEAR: STEPPING INTO YOUR BRAVE ZONE

Scripture: "For God hath not given us the spirit of fear; but of power, and of love, and of a sound mind." - 2 Timothy 1:7 (KJV)

2 Timothy 1:7 reassures us that God has not given us a spirit of fear but of power, love, and a sound mind. In overcoming fear, draw upon His strength and promises to step into your brave zone. As you

confront fears, anchor yourself in God's Word and prayer. Claim His promises of courage and trust in His unfailing love to embolden you to face every challenge with faith and confidence.

Prayer: Gracious God, help us to overcome fear with faith and courage. Fill us with Your power, love, and sound mind, empowering us to step boldly into the brave zone. May Your presence dispel all fear, and Your peace reign in our hearts. Amen.

DAY 207

HONORING SACRIFICE: REFLECTING ON SERVICE AND COMMITMENT

Scripture: "Greater love hath no man than this, that a man lay down his life for his friends." - John 15:13 (KJV)

John 15:13 highlights the ultimate sacrifice of laying down one's life for others. In reflecting on service and commitment, honor the sacrifices made by those who have served and continue to serve with dedication and courage. As you reflect, express gratitude for the sacrifices of service members, past and present. Through prayer and remembrance, honor their commitment to duty and uphold their legacy of service with reverence and respect.

Prayer: Heavenly Father, we thank You for the sacrifice of those who have served and continue to serve with courage and commitment.

May we honor their legacy with gratitude and reverence, striving to uphold the values of service and sacrifice. Amen.

DAY 208
STRENGTHENING BONDS WITH FELLOW SERVICE MEMBERS

Scripture: "Iron sharpeneth iron; so a man sharpeneth the countenance of his friend." - Proverbs 27:17 (KJV)

Proverbs 27:17 illustrates the value of sharpening one another through fellowship and camaraderie. In strengthening bonds with fellow service members, seek to encourage and uplift one another in faith and service. As you build relationships, foster a spirit of unity and support among fellow believers. Through prayer, fellowship, and mutual encouragement, strengthen bonds that sharpen and strengthen your faith and commitment to service.

Prayer: Gracious God, bless our relationships with fellow service members, strengthening us with unity and support. May we uplift and encourage one another in faith and service, sharpening and strengthening our commitment to You and to one another. Amen.

DAY 209

FINDING PURPOSE BEYOND THE UNIFORM:
EXPLORING LIFE'S MEANING

Scripture: "And whatsoever ye do, do it heartily, as to the Lord, and not unto men." - Colossians 3:23 (KJV)

Colossians 3:23 reminds us to do everything heartily as unto the Lord. In exploring life's meaning beyond the uniform, seek to find purpose and fulfillment in serving God and others with excellence and dedication. As you reflect on life's purpose, surrender your ambitions and desires to God, allowing Him to guide and direct your path. Through prayer and seeking His will, discover fulfillment in fulfilling His purposes for your life, both in and out of uniform.

Prayer: Heavenly Father, guide us in discovering purpose and meaning beyond the uniform. Help us to serve You and others with excellence and dedication, finding fulfillment in fulfilling Your purposes for our lives. May our lives bring glory to Your name. Amen.

DAY 210

HEALING FROM TRAUMA: THE PATH TO
WHOLENESS AND RESTORATION

Scripture: "He healeth the broken in heart, and bindeth up their wounds." - Psalm 147:3 (KJV)

Psalm 147:3 offers a comforting promise of God's healing for the brokenhearted and wounded. In the journey of healing from trauma, trust in His power to bring wholeness and restoration to your life. As you seek healing, entrust your pain and suffering to God, knowing that He is the ultimate healer. Through prayer, seek His comfort and restoration, allowing His love and grace to mend the broken places and bring healing to your soul.

Prayer: Gracious God, we thank You for Your promise to heal the broken hearted and bind up their wounds. Grant us Your comfort and restoration as we journey through the process of healing from trauma. May Your healing touch bring wholeness and peace to our hearts. Amen.

DAY 211
PRACTICING GRATITUDE: FINDING JOY IN EVERYDAY MOMENTS

Scripture: "In everything give thanks: for this is the will of God in Christ Jesus concerning you." - 1 Thessalonians 5:18 (KJV)

1 Thessalonians 5:18 encourages us to give thanks in everything, highlighting the importance of practicing gratitude in our daily lives. Even in the midst of challenges, there is always something to be grateful for. Gratitude transforms ordinary moments into opportunities for joy and appreciation. As you cultivate a spirit of

thankfulness, you'll find that even the smallest blessings become sources of joy and inspiration.

Prayer: Heavenly Father, teach us to cultivate a heart of gratitude in all circumstances. Help us to find joy in the everyday moments and to recognize Your goodness in every blessing. May our lives overflow with thanksgiving, bringing glory to Your name. Amen.

DAY 212
EMBRACING CHANGE: ADAPTING TO NEW CHALLENGES

Scripture: "Behold, I will do a new thing; now it shall spring forth; shall ye not know it? I will even make a way in the wilderness, and rivers in the desert." - Isaiah 43:19 (KJV)

Isaiah 43:19 reminds us that God is constantly doing new things in our lives, even in the midst of change and uncertainty. As we embrace change, we can trust in His faithfulness to make a way where there seems to be none.

Change can be daunting, but it also offers opportunities for growth and transformation. By surrendering to God's leading and trusting in His promises, we can navigate new challenges with confidence and hope.

Prayer: Gracious God, grant us the courage to embrace change and adapt to new challenges. Help us to trust in Your faithfulness and to recognize Your hand at work in every season of our lives. May we find strength and hope in You as we journey through times of change. Amen.

DAY 213
RESTORING HOPE: REDISCOVERING FAITH IN DIFFICULT TIMES

Scripture: "Why art thou cast down, O my soul? and why art thou disquieted within me? hope thou in God: for I shall yet praise him, who is the health of my countenance, and my God." - Psalm 42:11 (KJV)

Psalm 42:11 encourages us to place our hope in God, even in the midst of despair and uncertainty. When we feel overwhelmed by difficult times, we can find restoration and strength in trusting Him.

In times of struggle, turn to God in prayer and seek His presence. He is our source of hope and comfort, and He promises to sustain us through every trial. As we draw near to Him, our faith is renewed, and our hope is restored.

Prayer: Heavenly Father, in times of difficulty, restore our hope and strengthen our faith. Help us to trust in Your unfailing love and to find solace in Your presence. May we praise You even in the midst of adversity, knowing that You are our refuge and strength. Amen.

DAY 214

THE POWER OF FORGIVENESS: LETTING GO AND MOVING FORWARD

Scripture: "And be ye kind one to another, tenderhearted, forgiving one another, even as God for Christ's sake hath forgiven you." - Ephesians 4:32 (KJV)

Ephesians 4:32 reminds us of the power of forgiveness, both in receiving and extending it to others. Just as God has forgiven us through Christ, we are called to forgive others and release the burden of bitterness and resentment.

Forgiveness is a transformative act that frees us from the chains of anger and hurt. By choosing to forgive, we open our hearts to healing and restoration, allowing God's love to flow through us and bring reconciliation.

Prayer: Gracious God, grant us the strength to forgive as You have forgiven us. Help us to release the weight of bitterness and resentment, and to extend grace and compassion to those who have wronged us. May Your love and forgiveness flow through us, bringing healing and reconciliation. Amen.

DAY 215
CONNECTING WITH NATURE: FINDING SOLACE
IN THE OUTDOORS

Scripture: "The heavens declare the glory of God; and the firmament sheweth his handywork." - Psalm 19:1 (KJV)

Psalm 19:1 reflects on the majesty of God's creation, reminding us of His presence and power revealed in the natural world. When we connect with nature, we draw closer to the Creator and find solace in His handiwork.

Spending time outdoors offers opportunities for reflection, rejuvenation, and spiritual renewal. Whether it's marveling at the beauty of a sunset or listening to the rustle of leaves in the wind, nature speaks to our souls and invites us into communion with God.

Prayer: Heavenly Father, thank You for the beauty of Your creation that surrounds us. As we connect with nature, may we be reminded of Your presence and majesty. Renew our spirits and restore our souls as we find solace in the outdoors. Amen.

DAY 216
BALANCING DUTY AND PERSONAL WELLNESS:
PRIORITIZING SELF-CARE

Scripture: "Beloved, I wish above all things that thou mayest prosper and be in health, even as thy soul prospereth." - 3 John 1:2 (KJV)

3 John 1:2 emphasizes the importance of holistic well-being, both spiritually and physically. As we fulfill our duties, it's vital to prioritize self-care and maintain a healthy balance in our lives. Taking care of yourself is not selfish; it's essential for fulfilling your God-given purpose. Make time for rest, nourishment, and activities that bring you joy and refreshment. By caring for yourself, you'll be better equipped to serve others and honor God with your life.

Prayer: Gracious God, help us to prioritize self-care as we fulfill our duties and responsibilities. Grant us wisdom to find balance in our lives, caring for our physical, emotional, and spiritual well-being. May we honor You by caring for ourselves and serving others with strength and vitality. Amen.

DAY 217
COURAGEOUS LEADERSHIP: INSPIRING OTHERS THROUGH INTEGRITY AND COMPASSION

Scripture: "But be ye strong, and let not your hands be weak: for your work shall be rewarded." - 2 Chronicles 15:7 (KJV)

2 Chronicles 15:7 encourages us to be strong and steadfast in our leadership, knowing that our efforts will be rewarded. As leaders, we are called to inspire others through integrity, compassion, and unwavering faith. Courageous leadership requires humility, wisdom, and a heart for service. Lead by example, demonstrating integrity and compassion in all your interactions. Through your words and actions, inspire others to rise to their full potential and pursue excellence in all they do.

Prayer: Heavenly Father, grant us courage and wisdom as we lead others with integrity and compassion. May we inspire those around us to pursue excellence and to walk in the path of righteousness. Strengthen us for the task ahead, knowing that You are with us always. Amen.

DAY 218
EMBRACING DIVERSITY: CELEBRATING UNITY IN OUR DIFFERENCES

Scripture: "There is neither Jew nor Greek, there is neither bond nor free, there is neither male nor female: for ye are all one in Christ Jesus." - Galatians 3:28 (KJV)

Galatians 3:28 reminds us of the unity we share in Christ, transcending cultural, social, and gender differences. As followers of Christ, we are called to embrace diversity and celebrate the unique gifts and perspectives of every individual. Embracing diversity enriches our communities and strengthens our bonds as brothers and sisters in Christ. Instead of allowing differences to divide us, let us celebrate the beauty of God's diverse creation and work together in unity and love.

Prayer: Gracious God, help us to embrace diversity and celebrate unity in our differences. Open our hearts to appreciate the unique gifts and perspectives of every individual, and guide us in building communities of love and acceptance. May Your kingdom be a reflection of the diversity and unity found in Christ. Amen.

DAY 219
RESPECTING BOUNDARIES: SETTING HEALTHY LIMITS IN RELATIONSHIPS

Scripture: "A man's heart deviseth his way: but the Lord directeth his steps." - Proverbs 16:9 (KJV)

Proverbs 16:9 reminds us of God's sovereignty over our lives, including our relationships. As we navigate friendships, family dynamics, and professional connections, it's important to establish healthy boundaries guided by God's wisdom and direction. Respecting boundaries is essential for maintaining healthy relationships and honoring God's design for our lives. Set boundaries with love and clarity, communicating your needs and expectations while also respecting the boundaries of others. By doing so, you'll cultivate relationships built on mutual respect and trust.

Prayer: Heavenly Father, grant us wisdom to establish healthy boundaries in our relationships. Help us to communicate with love and clarity, honoring Your design for healthy, thriving connections. Guide us in respecting the boundaries of others while also protecting our own well-being. Amen.

DAY 220
EMBRACING VULNERABILITY: STRENGTH IN AUTHENTICITY

Scripture: "And he said unto me, My grace is sufficient for thee: for my strength is made perfect in weakness. Most gladly therefore will I rather glory in my infirmities, that the power of Christ may rest upon me." - 2 Corinthians 12:9 (KJV)

2 Corinthians 12:9 reminds us of the paradox of strength found in weakness. Embracing vulnerability allows us to experience the transformative power of God's grace and strength in our lives. Authenticity fosters deep connections with God and others, as we allow ourselves to be fully known and loved. Instead of hiding behind masks of perfection, embrace vulnerability as an opportunity for growth, healing, and intimacy with God and those around you.

Prayer: Gracious God, help us to embrace vulnerability as a pathway to experiencing Your grace and strength. May we find courage in authenticity, knowing that Your power is made perfect in our weakness. Empower us to live with open hearts and transparent lives, glorifying You in all we do. Amen.

DAY 221
FINDING STRENGTH IN SOLITUDE: CULTIVATING INNER PEACE

"Be still, and know that I am God: I will be exalted among the heathen, I will be exalted in the earth." - Psalm 46:10 (KJV)

In the midst of chaos and clamor, there lies a sanctuary in solitude, where the whispers of your soul find resonance with the divine. Embrace the silence, for it is in the quiet moments that you discover the depth of your strength. As a military man/woman, your days may be filled with noise and demands, but within you, there is a wellspring of peace waiting to be tapped. Just as Jesus withdrew to solitary places for communion with His Father, so too must you seek solace in the arms of your Creator. In the stillness, you will find clarity, courage, and the assurance that you are never alone. Let your heart be anchored in the unshakable peace that surpasses all understanding.

Prayer: Heavenly Father, in the solitude of this moment, I find refuge in Your presence. Grant me the strength to embrace the quiet and discover the peace that only You can provide. As I face the challenges ahead, may Your peace guard my heart and mind. Amen.

DAY 222

THE GIFT OF SERVICE: MAKING A DIFFERENCE IN THE LIVES OF OTHERS

"For even the Son of man came not to be ministered unto, but to minister, and to give his life a ransom for many." - Mark 10:45 (KJV)

In the uniform of service, you embody the essence of selflessness and sacrifice. As a military woman, your calling extends beyond the battlefield; it resonates in the lives you touch and the hearts you inspire. Embrace the privilege of service, for it is through giving that you receive the greatest blessings. Just as Christ laid down His life for humanity, so too are you called to pour out your life for the sake of others. Whether in acts of kindness, compassion, or courage, your service leaves an indelible mark on the world. Never underestimate the power of a single gesture to transform lives and illuminate hope in the darkest of times.

Prayer: Lord, teach me the true essence of service, that I may walk in the footsteps of Christ and shine Your light in the world. Grant me the grace to serve with humility, compassion, and unwavering love. May my life be a testament to Your goodness and grace. Amen.

DAY 223

EMBRACING UNCERTAINTY: TRUSTING THE JOURNEY AHEAD

"Trust in the Lord with all thine heart; and lean not unto thine own understanding. In all thy ways acknowledge him, and he shall direct thy paths." - Proverbs 3:5-6 (KJV)

In the ebb and flow of military life, uncertainty looms like a shadow, casting doubt upon the path ahead. Yet, in the midst of ambiguity, there is an anchor for the soul – trust in the unfailing wisdom and providence of God. Surrender your fears and uncertainties to Him, for He alone holds the blueprint of your life. Just as the Israelites trusted God to lead them through the wilderness, so too must you trust in His guidance through the unknown terrain of your journey. Though the road may be winding and fraught with challenges, rest assured that every step is ordained by the hand of your Heavenly Father.

Prayer: Heavenly Father, in the midst of uncertainty, I place my trust in You. Illuminate my path with Your wisdom and grace, that I may navigate the journey ahead with courage and conviction. Help me to surrender my fears and uncertainties to Your loving care, knowing that Your plans for me are good. Amen.

DAY 224

RENEWING MIND, BODY, AND SPIRIT: THE IMPORTANCE OF REST

"Come unto me, all ye that labour and are heavy laden, and I will give you rest." - Matthew 11:28 (KJV)

In the relentless rhythm of military life, rest is often deemed a luxury, overshadowed by the demands of duty. Yet, rest is not a sign of weakness, but rather a source of renewal for mind, body, and spirit. Just as God rested on the seventh day of creation, so too are you called to embrace the gift of rest.

Amidst the chaos and clamor, carve out moments of stillness to replenish your soul and recharge your spirit. For it is in the quietude of rest that you find strength to face the battles ahead. Surrender your burdens to the One who offers rest to the weary, and allow His peace to envelop you like a gentle embrace.

Prayer: Gracious God, in the busyness of life, grant me the wisdom to prioritize rest and renewal. Fill me with Your peace, that I may find rest for my soul amidst the storms of life. Help me to cease striving and trust in Your provision, knowing that in You, I find true rest. Amen.

DAY 225

OVERCOMING OBSTACLES: TURNING CHALLENGES INTO OPPORTUNITIES

"I can do all things through Christ which strengtheneth me." -
Philippians 4:13 (KJV)

As a military woman, you face obstacles and challenges on a daily basis, but within every obstacle lies an opportunity for growth and triumph. With Christ as your strength and guide, you possess the resilience and determination to overcome any adversity that comes your way. Just as David faced Goliath with unwavering faith, so too can you conquer giants in your path. Embrace challenges as stepping stones to greatness, knowing that each obstacle you overcome strengthens your character and deepens your faith. With Christ as your anchor, you can navigate the turbulent waters of life with courage and confidence, turning obstacles into opportunities for His glory.

Prayer: Heavenly Father, grant me the courage and strength to face obstacles with faith and perseverance. Help me to see challenges as opportunities for growth and transformation, knowing that You are with me every step of the way. Give me wisdom to discern Your will and courage to follow where You lead. Amen.

DAY 226
EMBRACING THE UNKNOWN: FAITH AS A SOURCE OF STRENGTH

"Now faith is the substance of things hoped for, the evidence of things not seen." - Hebrews 11:1 (KJV)

In the unpredictable journey of military life, the unknown stretches before you like an endless horizon. Yet, in the midst of uncertainty, faith becomes your steadfast anchor, grounding you in the assurance of God's promises. Just as Abraham journeyed into the unknown at God's command, so too must you step forward in faith, trusting in His unfailing guidance. Embrace the mystery of the future with courage and conviction, knowing that your Heavenly Father goes before you, paving the way with His grace and goodness. For where faith abounds, fear fades, and in the embrace of faith, you discover a wellspring of strength that sustains you through every trial and triumph.

Prayer: Lord, grant me unwavering faith to navigate the unknown with courage and confidence. May Your promises be my guiding light in the darkness, and Your presence my constant companion along the journey. Help me to trust in Your unfailing love and sovereignty, knowing that You hold the future in Your hands. Amen.

DAY 227
FINDING COMFORT IN RITUALS: NURTURING SPIRITUAL PRACTICES

"But his delight is in the law of the Lord; and in his law doth he meditate day and night." - Psalm 1:2 (KJV)

In the midst of the chaos and demands of military life, finding solace in spiritual practices can provide a sense of comfort and stability. Just as the psalmist found joy in meditating on the law of the Lord, so too can you find peace and nourishment for your soul in daily rituals of prayer, meditation, and reflection. Embrace the discipline of spiritual practices as a means of drawing closer to God and aligning your heart with His will. Whether it's starting your day with scripture reading, pausing for moments of prayer throughout the day, or ending your evening with gratitude, let these rituals anchor your soul and deepen your relationship with the Divine.

Prayer: Heavenly Father, as I engage in spiritual practices, may my heart be open to Your presence and my spirit attuned to Your voice. Help me to find comfort and strength in the rhythms of prayer, meditation, and reflection, knowing that in You, I find true rest for my soul. Amen.

DAY 228

FOSTERING RESILIENT FAMILIES: SUPPORTING LOVED ONES THROUGH DEPLOYMENT

"Two are better than one; because they have a good reward for their labour. For if they fall, the one will lift up his fellow: but woe to him that is alone when he falleth; for he hath not another to help him up." - Ecclesiastes 4:9-10 (KJV)

As a military woman, the journey of deployment can be arduous not only for you but also for your family. Yet, in the bond of love and unity, there is strength to weather the storms of separation. Just as the body of Christ supports and uplifts one another, so too must you rally around your loved ones, offering them the solace and support they need. Foster resilience within your family by cultivating open communication, fostering a spirit of adaptability, and nurturing a sense of unity and purpose. Together, you can navigate the challenges of deployment with grace and resilience, knowing that your bond as a family transcends distance and time.

Prayer: Heavenly Father, bless my family with strength and resilience as we navigate the challenges of deployment. Help us to lean on each other for support and encouragement, knowing that in unity, we find strength. Grant us Your peace and protection, and may our love for one another be a beacon of hope amidst the challenges we face. Amen.

DAY 229
CULTIVATING A WARRIOR SPIRIT: HARNESSING INNER STRENGTH

"Finally, my brethren, be strong in the Lord, and in the power of his might." - Ephesians 6:10 (KJV)

As a military woman, you are no stranger to adversity and challenge. Yet, within you lies a reservoir of strength waiting to be unleashed. Just as David faced Goliath with unwavering courage, so too can you harness your inner warrior spirit to conquer the battles before you. Cultivate resilience in the face of adversity by anchoring your identity in Christ, the source of your strength and courage. Equip yourself with the armor of God – the shield of faith, the helmet of salvation, the breastplate of righteousness – and stand firm against the schemes of the enemy.

Prayer: Lord, strengthen me with Your mighty power, that I may face the challenges before me with courage and conviction. Fill me with Your Spirit, that I may walk in the confidence of Your promises and the assurance of Your presence. Help me to cultivate a warrior spirit that fears no foe and trusts in Your unfailing protection. Amen.

DAY 230
THE POWER OF PERSPECTIVE: SHIFTING FROM FEAR TO FAITH

"For God hath not given us the spirit of fear; but of power, and of love, and of a sound mind." - 2 Timothy 1:7 (KJV)

In the crucible of military life, fear can often cloud your vision and paralyze your spirit. Yet, in the light of faith, fear fades into insignificance, replaced by the power, love, and sound mind that God has bestowed upon you. Choose to view the world through the lens of faith, for where fear sees obstacles, faith sees opportunities. Shift your perspective from fear to faith by fixing your eyes on the promises of God, rather than the uncertainties of the world. Embrace each challenge as an opportunity to grow in faith and dependence on the One who holds the future in His hands.

Prayer: Heavenly Father, banish fear from my heart and fill me with Your power, love, and sound mind. Help me to view the world through the lens of faith, trusting in Your goodness and sovereignty in all circumstances. Grant me the courage to step out in faith, knowing that You are with me always. Amen.

DAY 231
EMBRACING CHANGE: FINDING STABILITY IN TRANSITION

Scripture Reference: Isaiah 43:18-19 (KJV) "Remember ye not the former things, neither consider the things of old. Behold, I will do a new thing; now it shall spring forth; shall ye not know it? I will even make a way in the wilderness, and rivers in the desert."

In seasons of change, fear may grip your heart, and uncertainty may cloud your mind. But remember, dear warrior, change is the very essence of growth. Just as the seasons shift, so do the chapters of our lives. Yet, amidst the turmoil of transition, there is an unwavering anchor: the steadfast love of the Almighty. He who promises to make a way where there seems to be none. Embrace the winds of change, for they carry the fragrance of new beginnings. Stand firm upon the Rock of Ages, for His stability transcends the shifting sands of time. In every transition, find solace in His unchanging nature. His promises are your refuge, His presence your fortress.

Prayer: Heavenly Father, in the midst of life's transitions, grant me the grace to find stability in You. Help me to trust Your leading and embrace the changes with courage and faith. Amen.

DAY 232
WALKING IN PURPOSE: FULFILLING YOUR CALLING WITH COURAGE

Scripture Reference: Esther 4:14 (KJV) "For if thou altogether holdest thy peace at this time, then shall there enlargement and deliverance arise to the Jews from another place; but thou and thy father's house shall be destroyed: and who knoweth whether thou art come to the kingdom for such a time as this?"

In the heart of every warrior beats a purpose, a divine calling ordained by the Creator of the heavens and the earth. Like Esther, you are positioned for such a time as this. Your journey is not by chance, but by divine design. Courageously embrace your calling, knowing that within you lies the power to impact nations and change destinies. Though the path may be fraught with challenges, fear not, for He who has called you is faithful to sustain you.

Step into the arena of purpose with boldness and unwavering resolve. Let courage be your companion, and faith your guiding light. For in fulfilling your calling, you walk in alignment with the heartbeat of heaven.

Prayer: Lord, ignite within me the courage to walk boldly in the purpose You have ordained for my life. May I fulfill my calling with unwavering faith and steadfast courage, knowing that You go before me, guiding my every step. Amen.

DAY 233
EMBRACING IMPERFECTION: FINDING BEAUTY IN FLAWS

Scripture Reference: 2 Corinthians 12:9 (KJV) "And he said unto me, My grace is sufficient for thee: for my strength is made perfect in weakness. Most gladly therefore will I rather glory in my infirmities, that the power of Christ may rest upon me."

In a world that celebrates perfection, dare to embrace your imperfections as a canvas for divine grace. For it is in our weaknesses that the strength of the Almighty is made manifest. Release the burden of perfection, dear warrior, and embrace the beauty of your flaws. For it is through our brokenness that His light shines brightest. Your scars tell a story of redemption, your imperfections a testament to His unfailing love. In the tapestry of your life, each imperfection is a thread woven with purpose and intention. Let go of the illusion of perfection and embrace the beauty of authenticity. For it is in embracing our flaws that we find true freedom and wholeness.

Prayer: Heavenly Father, thank You for loving me in my imperfections and embracing me in my weaknesses. Help me to see the beauty in my flaws and to embrace them as a testament to Your grace. Amen.

DAY 234
STANDING TALL IN ADVERSITY: RESILIENCE IN THE FACE OF CHALLENGES

Scripture Reference: Psalm 46:1-3 (KJV) "God is our refuge and strength, a very present help in trouble. Therefore will not we fear, though the earth be removed, and though the mountains be carried into the midst of the sea; Though the waters thereof roar and be troubled, though the mountains shake with the swelling thereof. Selah."

In the crucible of adversity, you are forged into a warrior of resilience, strong and unyielding. Though the storms may rage and the winds may howl, fear not, for the Almighty is your refuge and strength. Stand tall, dear warrior, for you are not alone in the battle. The One who calms the storm walks beside you, His presence a shield against the fiery darts of the enemy. Though adversity may bend you, it shall not break you, for your roots are anchored deep in the soil of His love.

In the face of challenges, let resilience be your armor, and faith your sword. For you are more than a conqueror through Him who strengthens you. Stand firm, for victory is assured to those who trust in the Lord.

Prayer: Lord, in the midst of adversity, grant me the strength to stand firm and the resilience to persevere. Help me to trust in Your unfailing love, knowing that You are my refuge and strength in every trial. Amen.

DAY 235
RENEWING HOPE: FINDING LIGHT IN DARK TIMES

Scripture Reference: Romans 15:13 (KJV) "Now the God of hope fill you with all joy and peace in believing, that ye may abound in hope, through the power of the Holy Ghost."

In the darkest of nights, when despair threatens to engulf your soul, remember that hope is not lost, for the God of hope shines His light in the midst of darkness. Renew your hope, dear warrior, for His promises are steadfast and true. Though the night may be long, joy comes in the morning light. Lift your eyes to the heavens, for your help comes from the Maker of heaven and earth.

In the crucible of adversity, let hope be your anchor, and faith your guiding star. For He who promised is faithful to fulfill every word spoken over your life. Though the journey may be fraught with challenges, fear not, for the God of hope walks beside you, His light illuminating the path ahead.

Prayer: Heavenly Father, renew my hope in Your unfailing love, and fill me with joy and peace in believing. Help me to abound in hope through the power of Your Holy Spirit, knowing that You are faithful to fulfill Your promises. Amen.

DAY 236
CELEBRATING MILESTONES: REFLECTING ON GROWTH AND PROGRESS

Scripture Reference: Philippians 1:6 (KJV) "Being confident of this very thing, that he which hath begun a good work in you will perform it until the day of Jesus Christ."

As you journey through life's winding roads, take a moment to pause and reflect on the milestones you've achieved. For each victory, each triumph, is a testament to the faithfulness of the One who began a good work in you. Celebrate your milestones, dear warrior, for they are markers of growth and progress along the path of purpose. Though the road may be long and the journey arduous, take heart, for He who has called you is faithful to complete the work He has started.

In the tapestry of your life, each milestone is a thread woven with purpose and intention. Look back with gratitude, look forward with anticipation, for the best is yet to come. As you celebrate your milestones, may you be filled with renewed faith and unwavering hope for the journey ahead.

Prayer: Lord, thank You for the milestones I've achieved along the journey of life. Help me to celebrate each victory as a testament to Your faithfulness and to press forward with renewed faith and unwavering hope. Amen.

DAY 237
BUILDING BRIDGES: REACHING OUT ACROSS DIFFERENCES

Scripture Reference: Galatians 3:28 (KJV) "There is neither Jew nor Greek, there is neither bond nor free, there is neither male nor female: for ye are all one in Christ Jesus."

In a world divided by walls of prejudice and barriers of misunderstanding, dare to be a bridge builder, dear warrior. For in Christ, there is neither Jew nor Greek, neither bond nor free, neither male nor female. We are all one in Him. Reach out across differences, extending the hand of fellowship and the heart of compassion. For love knows no bounds, and grace knows no limits. Let unity be your anthem, and reconciliation your mission. In the tapestry of humanity, each thread is woven with the same divine purpose: to love and be loved. Break down the walls that divide, and build bridges of understanding and empathy. For in embracing diversity, we reflect the beauty of the One who created us in His image.

Prayer: Heavenly Father, help me to be a bridge builder in a world divided by walls of prejudice and barriers of misunderstanding. Fill me with Your love and grace, that I may reach out across differences with compassion and understanding. Amen.

DAY 238
THE STRENGTH OF COMMUNITY: FINDING SUPPORT IN TIMES OF NEED

Scripture Reference: Ecclesiastes 4:9-10 (KJV) "Two are better than one; because they have a good reward for their labour. For if they fall, the one will lift up his fellow: but woe to him that is alone when he falleth; for he hath not another to help him up."

In the crucible of life's trials, you need not walk alone, for you are surrounded by a community of warriors who stand ready to lift you up when you fall. Lean on the strength of community, dear warrior, for in unity there is power. Though the journey may be fraught with challenges, fear not, for you are not alone in the battle. In times of need, reach out to your fellow warriors, for they are your brothers and sisters in arms. Together, you are stronger, together, you are unstoppable. Let love be your bond, and unity your strength.

Prayer: Lord, thank You for the strength of community, for the brothers and sisters who stand by my side in times of need. Help me to lean on them for support and to be a source of strength and encouragement to others. Amen.

DAY 239
EMBRACING AUTHENTICITY: LIVING YOUR TRUTH WITH COURAGE

Scripture Reference: Psalm 139:14 (KJV) "I will praise thee; for I am fearfully and wonderfully made: marvellous are thy works; and that my soul knoweth right well."

In a world that demands conformity, dare to be authentically you, dear warrior. For you are fearfully and wonderfully made, a masterpiece crafted by the hands of the Almighty. Embrace your authenticity, for it is your superpower in a world filled with imitations. Let your light shine brightly, unapologetically, for you were created to stand out, not to blend in. In the tapestry of humanity, each thread is unique, each strand woven with purpose and intention. Embrace your uniqueness, dear warrior, and let it be a beacon of hope and inspiration to those around you.

Prayer: Heavenly Father, thank You for creating me fearfully and wonderfully. Help me to embrace my authenticity and to live my truth with courage and conviction. May my life be a reflection of Your glory and grace. Amen.

DAY 240
TRUSTING THE PROCESS: SURRENDERING TO DIVINE TIMING

Scripture Reference: Ecclesiastes 3:1 (KJV) "To everything there is a season, and a time to every purpose under the heaven."

In the tapestry of life, every thread is woven with divine purpose and intention. Though the journey may be fraught with twists and turns, trust in the One who holds the threads of your destiny in His hands. Surrender to divine timing, dear warrior, for His timing is perfect, His plans are flawless. Though the vision may tarry, wait patiently, for it shall surely come to pass. In the crucible of waiting, let patience be your virtue, and faith your anchor. For He who promised is faithful to fulfill every word spoken over your life. Trust the process, for in the fullness of time, His purposes will be revealed.

Prayer: Lord, help me to trust in Your perfect timing and to surrender to Your divine plan for my life. Give me the patience to wait for Your promises to be fulfilled and the faith to believe that Your plans are for my good. Amen.

DAY 241

HEALING WOUNDS: FINDING REDEMPTION AND RESTORATION

Scripture Reference: Psalm 147:3 (KJV) "He healeth the broken in heart, and bindeth up their wounds."

In the depths of your pain, know that there is a healer who tenderly binds up every wound. Like a skilled physician, He attends to the brokenness of your heart, bringing redemption and restoration to every wounded soul.

Turn to the One who bore your sorrows and carried your grief upon His shoulders. His love knows no bounds, His mercy endless. Let His healing touch soothe the ache within, bringing comfort to your weary soul. In the journey of healing, embrace the promise of redemption, dear warrior. For though the scars may remain, they bear witness to the miraculous work of the Great Physician. Trust in His faithfulness, and let His healing grace be your refuge and strength.

Prayer: Heavenly Father, heal the wounds of my heart and bring restoration to my soul. May Your tender touch bring comfort and peace to every broken area of my life. Amen.

DAY 242

THE POWER OF CONNECTION: BUILDING MEANINGFUL RELATIONSHIPS

Scripture Reference: Ecclesiastes 4:12 (KJV) "And if one prevail against him, two shall withstand him; and a threefold cord is not quickly broken."

In the tapestry of life, relationships are the threads that weave us together in unity and love. Embrace the power of connection, dear warrior, for in the company of kindred spirits, strength is multiplied, and burdens are lightened. Nurture meaningful relationships that edify the soul and uplift the spirit. Like a threefold cord, let your bonds be strong and unbreakable, rooted in love and mutual respect.

In the crucible of community, let compassion be your guide, and empathy your language. For in building meaningful relationships, you cultivate a sanctuary of love and acceptance where hearts find refuge and souls find solace.

Prayer: Lord, bless me with meaningful relationships that nourish my soul and uplift my spirit. Help me to cultivate connections rooted in love and mutual respect, that together, we may stand strong against the trials of life. Amen.

DAY 243

LIVING WITH PURPOSE: FINDING MEANING IN EVERYDAY ACTIONS

Scripture Reference: Colossians 3:17 (KJV) "And whatsoever ye do in word or deed, do all in the name of the Lord Jesus, giving thanks to God and the Father by him."

In the tapestry of your days, every moment is an opportunity to live with purpose and intention. Whether in the grand gestures or the mundane tasks, let every word and deed be a reflection of the love and grace of our Lord Jesus Christ. Find meaning in the everyday actions, dear warrior, for in serving others, you serve the One who gave His life as a ransom for many. Let your life be a living testimony to His goodness and mercy, shining brightly in a world darkened by despair.

In the crucible of purpose, let gratitude be your compass, and love your guiding light. For in living for His glory, you find fulfillment beyond measure, and joy unspeakable.

Prayer: Heavenly Father, help me to live with purpose and intention in every word and deed. May my life be a reflection of Your love and grace, bringing glory to Your name and blessing to those around me. Amen.

DAY 244

FINDING STRENGTH IN UNITY: SUPPORTING EACH OTHER AS A COMMUNITY

Scripture Reference: Acts 2:42-47 (KJV) "And they continued stedfastly in the apostles' doctrine and fellowship, and in breaking of bread, and in prayers."

In the fellowship of believers, there is strength beyond measure, for we are united by a common bond of love and faith. Like the early church, let us steadfastly support one another in times of joy and in times of need. Draw strength from the unity of community, dear warrior, for in the company of kindred spirits, burdens are shared, and victories celebrated. Let love be your banner, and compassion your creed, as you journey together in the footsteps of our Lord. In the crucible of unity, let humility be your mantle, and grace your garment. For in supporting one another, we fulfil the law of Christ and bear witness to His abiding presence among us.

Prayer: Lord, unite us as a community of believers, bound together by a common bond of love and faith. Strengthen us to support one another in times of joy and in times of need, that together, we may glorify Your name and advance Your kingdom. Amen.

DAY 245
RESILIENCE IN GRIEF: FINDING HOPE IN TIMES OF LOSS

Scripture Reference: Psalm 34:18 (KJV) "The Lord is nigh unto them that are of a broken heart; and saveth such as be of a contrite spirit."

In the valley of grief, know that you are not alone, for the Lord is near to the brokenhearted and saves those who are crushed in spirit. Though the shadows may deepen and the night may seem endless, His light shines brightly, bringing hope to the darkest of days. Find resilience in the embrace of His love, dear warrior, for His grace is sufficient to carry you through every trial and tribulation. Let His comfort be your solace, and His peace your anchor, as you navigate the tumultuous waters of grief.

In the crucible of loss, let faith be your shield, and hope your compass. For though the journey may be fraught with pain, joy comes in the morning light, and beauty rises from the ashes of despair.

Prayer: Heavenly Father, comfort the hearts of those who mourn, and bring hope to the brokenhearted. May Your presence be a source of strength and solace in times of grief, and Your love a beacon of light in the darkness. Amen.

DAY 246
EMBRACING CHANGE: EMBRACING THE JOURNEY OF TRANSFORMATION

Scripture Reference: Romans 12:2 (KJV) "And be not conformed to this world: but be ye transformed by the renewing of your mind, that ye may prove what is that good, and acceptable, and perfect, will of God."

In the crucible of change, embrace the journey of transformation, dear warrior, for in the renewing of your mind, you discover the will of God for your life. Though the path may be unfamiliar and the future uncertain, fear not, for He who called you is faithful to complete the work He has started. Embrace change as a catalyst for growth and renewal, for in every season of transition, there is an opportunity for transformation. Let go of the old and embrace the new, trusting in the sovereignty of the One who holds the future in His hands.

In the crucible of transformation, let faith be your guide, and courage your companion. For though the journey may be daunting, the destination is glorious, as you become more and more like the One who called you out of darkness into His marvelous light.

Prayer: Lord, guide me through the journey of transformation, and renew my mind according to Your perfect will. May I embrace change with faith and courage, trusting in Your faithfulness to complete the work You have started in me. Amen.

DAY 247
THE PATH TO FORGIVENESS: RELEASING RESENTMENT AND FINDING PEACE

Scripture Reference: Ephesians 4:32 (KJV) "And be ye kind one to another, tenderhearted, forgiving one another, even as God for Christ's sake hath forgiven you."

In the crucible of forgiveness, find the path to peace, dear warrior, for in releasing resentment, you free yourself from the chains of bitterness and find healing for your soul. Though the wounds may run deep and the pain may linger, choose to forgive as you have been forgiven by our gracious God. Follow the example of Christ, who bore the sins of the world upon His shoulders and extended forgiveness to all who would receive it. Let kindness be your cloak, and tender-heartedness your hallmark, as you extend grace to those who have wronged you.

In the crucible of forgiveness, let love be your guide, and mercy your compass. For in releasing others from the debt they owe you, you discover the true meaning of freedom and find peace that surpasses all understanding.

Prayer: Heavenly Father, grant me the strength to forgive as You have forgiven me, and to release resentment from my heart. Help me to extend grace and mercy to those who have wronged me, that I may experience the peace that surpasses all understanding. Amen.

DAY 248

COURAGEOUS CONVERSATIONS: SPEAKING TRUTH WITH LOVE

Scripture Reference: Ephesians 4:15 (KJV) "But speaking the truth in love, may grow up into him in all things, which is the head, even Christ."

In the crucible of communication, speak the truth in love, dear warrior, for in doing so, you grow in maturity and likeness to Christ. Though the words may be difficult to utter and the conversation uncomfortable, let love be your motivation, and truth your guiding principle. Follow the example of our Lord Jesus Christ, who spoke truth with compassion and confronted sin with grace. Let your words be seasoned with salt, and your speech seasoned with grace, as you seek to build up and edify those around you. In the crucible of conversation, let wisdom be your counsel, and discernment your shield. For in speaking the truth in love, you pave the way for reconciliation and healing, and point others to the One who is the Way, the Truth, and the Life.

Prayer: Lord, grant me the courage to speak the truth in love, and the wisdom to do so with grace and compassion. May my words build up and edify others, pointing them to You, the source of all truth and love. Amen.

DAY 249

NURTURING RESILIENT CHILDREN:
SUPPORTING MILITARY FAMILIES

Scripture Reference: Proverbs 22:6 (KJV) "Train up a child in the way he should go: and when he is old, he will not depart from it."

In the crucible of parenting, nurture resilient children by anchoring them in the timeless truths of God's Word. As members of military families, they face unique challenges and uncertainties, but through your guidance and example, they can find strength and resilience in the midst of adversity. Train up your children in the ways of righteousness and honor, instilling in them the values of courage, perseverance, and faith. Let your home be a sanctuary of love and stability, where they can find refuge in the midst of life's storms.

In the crucible of parenting, let patience be your virtue, and love your guiding principle. For in nurturing resilient children, you leave a lasting legacy of faith and fortitude that will endure for generations to come.

Prayer: Heavenly Father, bless our military families with wisdom and grace as they navigate the challenges of parenting. Help us to nurture resilient children who are anchored in Your Word and equipped to face whatever challenges come their way. Amen.

DAY 250
EMBRACING UNCERTAINTY: FINDING
STABILITY IN THE UNKNOWN

Scripture Reference: Isaiah 41:10 (KJV) "Fear thou not; for I am with thee: be not dismayed; for I am thy God: I will strengthen thee; yea, I will help thee; yea, I will uphold thee with the right hand of my righteousness."

In the crucible of uncertainty, find stability in the unchanging promises of God, dear warrior. Though the future may be veiled in shadows and the path ahead obscured, fear not, for the Almighty is your refuge and strength. Embrace uncertainty as an opportunity to deepen your faith and trust in the One who holds the future in His hands. Let your heart be steadfast, and your spirit unshaken, as you lean on His everlasting arms.

In the crucible of uncertainty, let faith be your anchor, and hope your compass. For in trusting in the sovereignty of God, you discover a peace that surpasses all understanding, and a stability that endures through every storm.

Prayer: Lord, in the midst of uncertainty, help me to trust in Your unchanging character and steadfast love. Strengthen me with Your presence and uphold me with Your righteous right hand, that I may find stability in the midst of the unknown. Amen.

DAY 251

FINDING STRENGTH IN FAITH: TRUSTING IN GOD'S PLAN

Scripture Reference: Isaiah 41:13 (KJV) "For I the Lord thy God will hold thy right hand, saying unto thee, Fear not; I will help thee."

In the crucible of life's trials, find strength in the unwavering promises of God. Though the storms may rage and the winds may howl, fear not, for the Almighty holds you securely in the palm of His hand. Trust in God's plan, dear warrior, for His ways are higher than our ways, and His thoughts are higher than our thoughts. Though the path may be obscured and the future uncertain, rest assured that He who promised is faithful to fulfill every word spoken over your life. In the crucible of faith, let trust be your anchor, and hope your compass. For in leaning not on your own understanding but acknowledging Him in all your ways, you discover a peace that surpasses all understanding.

Prayer: Heavenly Father, grant me the strength to trust in Your plan, even when the path ahead is unclear. Help me to rest in Your promises and find peace in Your presence, knowing that You hold my future securely in Your hands. Amen.

DAY 252

EMBRACING CREATIVITY: FINDING SOLUTIONS AMIDST CHALLENGES

Scripture Reference: Exodus 35:31 (KJV) "And he hath filled him with the spirit of God, in wisdom, in understanding, and in knowledge, and in all manner of workmanship."

In the crucible of challenges, unleash the power of creativity, for the spirit of God dwells within you, equipping you with wisdom and understanding to overcome every obstacle that stands in your way. Embrace creativity as a divine gift, dear warrior, for in thinking outside the box and exploring new possibilities, you discover innovative solutions to even the most daunting of challenges. Let your imagination soar, and your creativity flow, as you tap into the limitless resources of the Creator of the heavens and the earth. In the crucible of creativity, let faith be your guide, and courage your companion. For in trusting in the One who has called you, you find strength to face every trial and triumph over every tribulation.

Prayer: Lord, fill me with Your spirit of creativity and wisdom, that I may find solutions to the challenges I face. Help me to think outside the box and explore new possibilities, trusting in Your guidance every step of the way. Amen.

DAY 253

THE POWER OF POSITIVITY: CULTIVATING AN OPTIMISTIC MINDSET

Scripture Reference: Philippians 4:8 (KJV) "Finally, brethren, whatsoever things are true, whatsoever things are honest, whatsoever things are just, whatsoever things are pure, whatsoever things are lovely, whatsoever things are of good report; if there be any virtue, and if there be any praise, think on these things."

In the crucible of negativity, cultivate the power of positivity, for your thoughts have the power to shape your reality and transform your circumstances. Set your mind on things above, dear warrior, for in dwelling on that which is true, honorable, and praiseworthy, you discover the beauty and goodness that surround you. Embrace positivity as a mindset, a way of seeing the world through the lens of faith and hope. Though the storms may rage and the shadows may loom large, choose to focus on the light that pierces through the darkness and illuminates the path ahead.

In the crucible of positivity, let gratitude be your attitude, and joy your disposition. For in cultivating an optimistic mindset, you unlock the door to endless possibilities and experience the fullness of life that God intends for you.

Prayer: Heavenly Father, help me to cultivate a positive mindset and set my thoughts on things above. Fill me with gratitude and joy, that I may experience the abundance of life that You have promised to those who trust in You. Amen.

DAY 254
RESILIENCE IN THE FACE OF LOSS: FINDING COMFORT IN MEMORIES

Scripture Reference: Psalm 30:5 (KJV) "For his anger endureth but a moment; in his favour is life: weeping may endure for a night, but joy cometh in the morning."

In the crucible of loss, find resilience in the comforting embrace of cherished memories, for though the night may be long and the tears may flow freely, joy comes in the morning light, bringing healing and restoration to the wounded soul. Treasure the memories of your loved ones, dear warrior, for in remembering their legacy and honoring their life, you find solace in the midst of grief. Though their physical presence may be gone, their spirit lives on in the hearts of those who loved them. In the crucible of loss, let faith be your anchor, and hope your compass. For in trusting in the promise of resurrection and reunion, you find comfort in the knowledge that one day, you will be reunited with your loved ones in the presence of the One who is the source of all comfort and peace.

Prayer: Lord, comfort me in my grief and surround me with Your presence. Help me to treasure the memories of my loved ones and find solace in the knowledge of Your promise of resurrection and reunion. Amen.

DAY 255

EMBRACING GRATITUDE: RECOGNIZING BLESSINGS IN DISGUISE

Scripture Reference: 1 Thessalonians 5:18 (KJV) "In everything give thanks: for this is the will of God in Christ Jesus concerning you."

In the crucible of adversity, cultivate the spirit of gratitude, for in giving thanks in all circumstances, you acknowledge the goodness and faithfulness of God, even in the midst of trials and tribulations. Embrace gratitude as a way of life, dear warrior, for in counting your blessings and recognizing the abundance of grace that surrounds you, you discover joy and contentment that transcends your circumstances. Though the storms may rage and the winds may howl, let thanksgiving be your song, and praise your offering. In the crucible of gratitude, let faith be your foundation, and love your motivation. For in giving thanks in all things, you align your heart with the will of God and open the floodgates of heaven to pour out His blessings upon you.

Prayer: Heavenly Father, teach me to cultivate a spirit of gratitude in all circumstances, knowing that You are faithful and Your love endures forever. Fill me with joy and contentment as I count my blessings and give thanks for Your goodness and grace. Amen.

DAY 256
BUILDING RESILIENT TEAMS: FOSTERING CAMARADERIE AND UNITY

Scripture Reference: Ecclesiastes 4:9-10 (KJV) "Two are better than one; because they have a good reward for their labour. For if they fall, the one will lift up his fellow: but woe to him that is alone when he falleth; for he hath not another to help him up."

In the crucible of teamwork, foster camaraderie and unity, for together, you are stronger, and together, you can overcome even the greatest of challenges that stand in your way. Build resilient teams, dear warrior, for in the company of kindred spirits and like-minded individuals, you find strength and support to face the trials and triumphs of life. Let love be your bond, and unity your strength, as you journey together in pursuit of a common goal. In the crucible of teamwork, let humility be your mantle, and grace your garment. For in lifting up one another and bearing each other's burdens, you fulfill the law of Christ and bear witness to His abiding presence among you.

Prayer: Lord, unite us as a team, bound together by a common bond of love and unity. Strengthen us to support one another in times of need and to celebrate each other's victories as our own. May our teamwork be a testament to Your faithfulness and grace. Amen.

DAY 257

FINDING BALANCE: PRIORITIZING MENTAL, PHYSICAL, AND EMOTIONAL HEALTH

Scripture Reference: 1 Corinthians 6:19-20 (KJV) "What? know ye not that your body is the temple of the Holy Ghost which is in you, which ye have of God, and ye are not your own? For ye are bought with a price: therefore glorify God in your body, and in your spirit, which are God's."

In the crucible of life's demands, find balance by prioritizing your mental, physical, and emotional health, for you are fearfully and wonderfully made, and your body is the temple of the Holy Spirit. Nurture your mental health, dear warrior, by guarding your thoughts and renewing your mind with the truth of God's Word. Let faith be your shield against anxiety and worry, and trust in the Lord to provide for all your needs according to His riches in glory.

Cultivate your physical health by honoring your body as a sacred vessel entrusted to you by God. Eat nourishing foods, exercise regularly, and rest in the assurance that your strength comes from the Lord, who gives power to the faint and increases the strength of the weak. Attend to your emotional health by expressing your feelings openly and seeking support from trusted friends and loved ones. Let vulnerability be your strength, and authenticity your hallmark, as you journey through the highs and lows of life with grace and resilience.

Prayer: Heavenly Father, grant me wisdom to prioritize my mental, physical, and emotional health, knowing that my body is a temple of the Holy Spirit. Help me to glorify You in all that I do, honoring You with my thoughts, words, and actions. Amen.

DAY 258
EMBRACING CHANGE: FINDING STRENGTH IN ADAPTABILITY

Scripture Reference: Isaiah 43:18-19 (KJV) "Remember ye not the former things, neither consider the things of old. Behold, I will do a new thing; now it shall spring forth; shall ye not know it? I will even make a way in the wilderness, and rivers in the desert." In the crucible of change, find strength in the promise of new beginnings, for the Lord is doing a new thing in your life, making a way where there seems to be no way.

Embrace change as an opportunity for growth and transformation, dear warrior, for though the journey may be fraught with uncertainty and discomfort, trust in the One who holds the future in His hands. Let go of the past and step boldly into the unknown, knowing that He who called you is faithful to complete the work He has started in you. In the crucible of change, let faith be your compass, and courage your guide. For in embracing the new thing that God is doing, you discover the beauty and wonder of His unfolding plan for your life.

Prayer: Lord, help me to embrace change with faith and courage, knowing that You are doing a new thing in my life. Give me strength to let go of the past and step boldly into the future, trusting in Your faithfulness to lead me every step of the way. Amen.

DAY 259
THE JOURNEY OF SELF-DISCOVERY: EXPLORING PERSONAL GROWTH

Scripture Reference: Proverbs 19:8 (KJV) "He that getteth wisdom loveth his own soul: he that keepeth understanding shall find good."

In the crucible of self-discovery, embark on a journey of personal growth and transformation, for in seeking wisdom and understanding, you uncover the depths of your soul and discover the goodness that lies within. Commit to lifelong learning, dear warrior, for the pursuit of knowledge is the pathway to growth and enlightenment. Let humility be your teacher, and curiosity your guide, as you explore the vast expanse of wisdom that awaits you. In the crucible of self-discovery, let reflection be your companion, and introspection your tool. For in examining your thoughts, beliefs, and behaviors, you uncover the areas in need of refinement and transformation, and forge a path toward becoming the best version of yourself.

Prayer: Heavenly Father, grant me wisdom and understanding as I embark on the journey of self-discovery and personal growth. Help me to love my soul by seeking after knowledge and understanding, and to find joy and fulfillment in the process of becoming more like You. Amen.

DAY 260
OVERCOMING SELF-DOUBT: CULTIVATING CONFIDENCE AND SELF-ESTEEM

Scripture Reference: Psalm 139:14 (KJV) "I will praise thee; for I am fearfully and wonderfully made: marvellous are thy works; and that my soul knoweth right well."

In the crucible of self-doubt, embrace the truth of your identity as a fearfully and wonderfully made child of God, for you are a masterpiece crafted by the hands of the Almighty. Cultivate confidence and self-esteem, dear warrior, by embracing the unique gifts and talents that God has bestowed upon you. Let go of comparison and perfectionism, and celebrate the beauty and uniqueness of who you are. In the crucible of self-doubt, let faith be your shield, and affirmation your sword. For in anchoring your identity in Christ and affirming the truth of His Word, you silence the voice of doubt and step boldly into the purpose and destiny that God has ordained for your life.

Prayer: Lord, help me to overcome self-doubt by anchoring my identity in You and embracing the truth of Your Word. Fill me with confidence and self-esteem, knowing that I am fearfully and wonderfully made in Your image. Amen.

DAY 261
THE POWER OF PRAYER: SEEKING GUIDANCE AND COMFORT

Scripture Reference: Philippians 4:6-7 (KJV) "Be careful for nothing; but in everything by prayer and supplication with thanksgiving let your requests be made known unto God. And the peace of God, which passeth all understanding, shall keep your hearts and minds through Christ Jesus."

In the crucible of life's trials, find solace and strength in the power of prayer, dear warrior. As the apostle Paul instructs, let your petitions be made known unto God with thanksgiving, and His peace, which surpasses all understanding, will guard your heart and mind in Christ Jesus. Like a child running into the arms of a loving parent, pour out your heart before the Lord, knowing that He hears your cries and collects your tears in His bottle. In the secret place of prayer, find refuge from the storms of life and discover the guidance and comfort that only He can provide. In the crucible of prayer, let faith be your anchor, and trust your compass. For in seeking God's guidance and comfort, you open the door to a deeper intimacy with the One who knows you intimately and cares for you deeply.

Prayer: Heavenly Father, thank You for the privilege of prayer, through which we can seek Your guidance and find comfort in times of need. Help us to approach Your throne with confidence, knowing that You hear our prayers and respond with grace and mercy. Amen.

DAY 262
CULTIVATING RESILIENCE: TURNING SETBACKS INTO COMEBACKS

Scripture Reference: James 1:2-4 (KJV) "My brethren, count it all joy when ye fall into divers temptations; Knowing this, that the trying of your faith worketh patience. But let patience have her perfect work, that ye may be perfect and entire, wanting nothing."

In the crucible of setbacks, cultivate resilience and perseverance, dear warrior. Though the trials may be many and the road may be rocky, count it all joy, knowing that the testing of your faith produces endurance. As James writes, "Let perseverance finish its work so that you may be mature and complete, not lacking anything." Let this truth be your motivation as you face adversity head-on, knowing that every setback is an opportunity for a comeback in the strength of the Lord.

Like a phoenix rising from the ashes, let your setbacks become the fuel for your comeback, as you trust in the faithfulness of God to bring beauty from ashes and strength from weakness. In the crucible of resilience, let hope be your anchor, and determination your compass. For in turning setbacks into comebacks, you discover the power to overcome every obstacle and the resilience to rise stronger than before.

Prayer: Lord, grant us the resilience to turn setbacks into comebacks, trusting in Your faithfulness to bring beauty from ashes and strength from weakness. Help us to count it all joy when we face trials, knowing that they produce endurance and maturity in our faith. Amen.

DAY 263
EMBRACING DIVERSITY: CELEBRATING DIFFERENCES AND BUILDING BRIDGES

Scripture Reference: Galatians 3:28 (KJV) "There is neither Jew nor Greek, there is neither bond nor free, there is neither male nor female: for ye are all one in Christ Jesus."

In the crucible of diversity, embrace the beauty of God's creation, dear warrior. For in Christ, there is no distinction between Jew or Greek, slave or free, male or female—all are one in Him. As the apostle Paul declares, "For as many of you as have been baptized into Christ have put on Christ." Let this truth be your guide as you celebrate the rich tapestry of cultures, backgrounds, and experiences that make up the body of Christ.

In the crucible of diversity, let love be your language, and unity your goal. For in embracing the differences among us, we build bridges of understanding and empathy, fostering a community where all are valued and respected.

Prayer: Heavenly Father, help us to embrace the diversity within Your body, celebrating the differences that make us unique while recognizing our unity in Christ. Guide us to build bridges of understanding and empathy, that Your love may be reflected in all we do. Amen.

DAY 264
FINDING PURPOSE IN SERVICE: MAKING A MEANINGFUL IMPACT

Scripture Reference: Mark 10:45 (KJV) "For even the Son of man came not to be ministered unto, but to minister, and to give his life a ransom for many."

In the crucible of service, find purpose and fulfillment in making a meaningful impact, dear warrior. Follow the example of our Lord Jesus Christ, who came not to be served, but to serve, and to give His life as a ransom for many. As Jesus teaches, "Whoever wants to become great among you must be your servant." Let this truth be your guiding principle as you seek to make a difference in the lives of others, serving with humility and compassion.

In the crucible of service, let love be your motivation, and selflessness your goal. For in pouring out your life for the sake of others, you discover the true meaning of greatness and leave a lasting legacy that echoes throughout eternity.

Prayer: Lord, teach us to find purpose and fulfillment in serving others, following the example of Your Son, Jesus Christ. Help us to embrace the call to serve with humility and compassion, making a meaningful impact in the lives of those around us. Amen.

DAY 265
RESILIENCE IN RELATIONSHIPS: NURTURING CONNECTIONS THROUGH CHALLENGES

Scripture Reference: Proverbs 17:17 (KJV) "A friend loveth at all times, and a brother is born for adversity."

In the crucible of relationships, cultivate resilience and strength, dear warrior. For true friendship is tested in the fires of adversity, and a faithful friend is like a sturdy shelter in the midst of life's storms. As the writer of Proverbs wisely observes, "A friend loves at all times, and a brother is born for a time of adversity." Let this truth be your anchor as you navigate the ups and downs of relationships, knowing that true bonds are forged in the crucible of challenges.

In the crucible of resilience, let forgiveness be your foundation, and love your guide. For in nurturing connections through the trials of life, you discover the depth of character and the richness of community that only adversity can reveal.

Prayer: Heavenly Father, grant us the strength to cultivate resilience in our relationships, loving one another at all times and standing firm as faithful friends through every trial. Help us to forgive as You have forgiven us, and to love as You have loved us. Amen.

DAY 266
EMBRACING VULNERABILITY: FINDING STRENGTH IN AUTHENTICITY

Scripture Reference: 2 Corinthians 12:9-10 (KJV) "And he said unto me, My grace is sufficient for thee: for my strength is made perfect in weakness. Most gladly therefore will I rather glory in my infirmities, that the power of Christ may rest upon me. Therefore, I take pleasure in infirmities, in reproaches, in necessities, in persecutions, in distresses for Christ's sake: for when I am weak, then am I strong."

In the crucible of vulnerability, find strength and courage in embracing your authentic self, dear warrior. For it is in our weaknesses that the power of Christ is made perfect, and His grace is sufficient to carry us through every trial. As the apostle Paul declares, "For when I am weak, then am I strong." Let this truth be your comfort as you lay bare your heart before the Lord and before others, knowing that He delights in your vulnerability and uses it for His glory. In the crucible of authenticity, let humility be your mantle, and transparency your strength. For in embracing vulnerability, you discover the freedom to be fully known and fully loved, just as you are.

Prayer: Lord, grant us the courage to embrace vulnerability, knowing that Your grace is sufficient for us and Your strength is made perfect in our weakness. Help us to find strength and courage in authenticity, laying bare our hearts before You and before others. Amen.

DAY 267
THE ART OF COMMUNICATION: BUILDING STRONGER CONNECTIONS

Scripture Reference: Proverbs 18:21 (KJV) "Death and life are in the power of the tongue: and they that love it shall eat the fruit thereof."

In the crucible of communication, wield the power of your words with wisdom and grace, dear warrior. For the tongue has the power to build up or tear down, to bring life or to bring death, and those who love it will eat the fruit of their words. As the writer of Proverbs observes, "Death and life are in the power of the tongue." Let this truth be your guide as you seek to build stronger connections through your words, choosing to speak life and encouragement to those around you. In the crucible of communication, let love be your motivation, and empathy your guide. For in listening with compassion and speaking with kindness, you create a space where hearts are opened and relationships are strengthened.

Prayer: Heavenly Father, help us to wield the power of our words with wisdom and grace, using them to build up and encourage those around us. Guide us to communicate with love and empathy, that we may build stronger connections and reflect Your heart to the world. Amen.

DAY 268

FINDING PEACE IN CHAOS: CULTIVATING CALM AMIDST TURBULENCE

Scripture Reference: Isaiah 26:3 (KJV) "Thou wilt keep him in perfect peace, whose mind is stayed on thee: because he trusteth in thee."

In the crucible of chaos, find perfect peace in the presence of the Lord, dear warrior. For He alone is our refuge and strength, a very present help in times of trouble, and His peace surpasses all understanding. As Isaiah writes, "You will keep in perfect peace those whose minds are steadfast, because they trust in you." Let this truth be your anchor in the midst of life's storms, as you fix your eyes on Jesus and trust in His unfailing love. In the crucible of chaos, let faith be your shield, and trust your fortress. For in cultivating a heart that is steadfast and secure in the Lord, you discover the calm that can only be found in His presence, even in the midst of turbulence.

Prayer: Lord, keep us in perfect peace as we fix our minds on You and trust in Your unfailing love. Help us to find calm amidst the chaos of life, knowing that You are our refuge and strength, a very present help in times of trouble. Amen.

DAY 269
OVERCOMING ADVERSITY: RISING STRONGER AFTER SETBACKS

Scripture Reference: Romans 8:28 (KJV) "And we know that all things work together for good to them that love God, to them who are the called according to his purpose."

In the crucible of adversity, find hope and assurance in the promise of God's providence, dear warrior. For He works all things together for the good of those who love Him and are called according to His purpose. As the apostle Paul declares, "We know that in all things God works for the good of those who love him, who have been called according to his purpose." Let this truth be your anchor as you face setbacks and trials, knowing that God is at work behind the scenes, orchestrating His perfect plan for your life. In the crucible of adversity, let perseverance be your virtue, and faith your strength. For in overcoming obstacles and rising stronger after setbacks, you discover the resilience and fortitude that can only be found in Christ.

Prayer: Heavenly Father, thank You for the assurance that You work all things together for our good, according to Your perfect plan. Help us to trust in Your providence, even in the midst of adversity, knowing that You are at work in our lives. Amen.

DAY 270
EMBRACING FORGIVENESS: HEALING WOUNDS AND MOVING FORWARD

Scripture Reference: Colossians 3:13 (KJV) "Forbearing one another, and forgiving one another, if any man have a quarrel against any: even as Christ forgave you, so also do ye."

In the crucible of forgiveness, find healing and freedom in extending grace to others, dear warrior. For just as Christ forgave you, so too are you called to forgive those who have wronged you, releasing the burden of bitterness and resentment that weighs heavy on your soul. As Paul admonishes, "Bear with each other and forgive one another if any of you has a grievance against someone. Forgive as the Lord forgave you."

Let this truth be your guide as you choose to extend mercy and compassion to those who have hurt you, following the example of our

Savior. In the crucible of forgiveness, let love be your motivation, and reconciliation your goal. For in choosing to forgive, you not only set yourself free from the chains of unforgiveness but also create space for healing and restoration in your relationships.

Prayer: Lord, grant us the grace to forgive as You have forgiven us, releasing the burden of bitterness and resentment that weighs heavy on our souls. Help us to extend mercy and compassion to those who have wronged us, that we may experience healing and freedom in You. Amen.

DAY 271
THE POWER OF MINDFULNESS: LIVING IN THE PRESENT MOMENT

Scripture Reference: Matthew 6:34 (KJV) "Take therefore no thought for the morrow: for the morrow shall take thought for the things of itself. Sufficient unto the day is the evil thereof."

In the crucible of mindfulness, discover the peace and clarity that come from living in the present moment, dear warrior. As Jesus teaches, do not worry about tomorrow, for each day has enough trouble of its own. Imagine standing by the shores of Galilee, feeling the warmth of the sun on your face and the gentle breeze rustling through your hair. In that moment, there is no past to regret or future to fear, only the beauty of the present moment unfolding before you. In the crucible of mindfulness, let gratitude be your guide and awareness your practice. For in cultivating a heart that is fully present, you awaken to the wonder and blessings that surround you each day, filling your soul with peace and contentment.

Prayer: Heavenly Father, help us to embrace the power of mindfulness, living fully in the present moment and trusting in Your provision for each day. Grant us the grace to let go of worries about the future and to find peace in Your presence here and now. Amen.

DAY 272
CULTIVATING RESILIENT FAMILIES: SUPPORTING EACH OTHER THROUGH TOUGH TIMES

Scripture Reference: Proverbs 22:6 (KJV) "Train up a child in the way he should go: and when he is old, he will not depart from it."

In the crucible of family, cultivate resilience and strength, dear warrior. As the writer of Proverbs advises, train up your children in the ways of the Lord, instilling in them values of faith, love, and perseverance that will serve as their anchor in times of trial. Imagine the warmth of a family gathered around the dinner table, sharing laughter and tears, joys and sorrows. In that sacred space, there is a bond that transcends the storms of life, a bond forged in love and strengthened by adversity. In the crucible of family, let patience be your virtue and forgiveness your practice. For in supporting and uplifting one another through tough times, you create a foundation of resilience that withstands the fiercest of storms and emerges stronger than before.

Prayer: Lord, bless our families with resilience and strength, that we may support and uplift one another through the trials of life. Help us to cultivate a bond that is rooted in love and strengthened by faith, trusting in Your provision and guidance every step of the way. Amen.

DAY 273
EMBRACING CHANGE: EMBRACING OPPORTUNITIES FOR GROWTH

Scripture Reference: Isaiah 43:18-19 (KJV) "Remember ye not the former things, neither consider the things of old. Behold, I will do a new thing; now it shall spring forth; shall ye not know it? I will even make a way in the wilderness, and rivers in the desert."

In the crucible of change, embrace the opportunities for growth and transformation, dear warrior. As the prophet Isaiah proclaims, God is constantly doing a new thing, making a way in the wilderness and rivers in the desert of our lives. Imagine standing at the edge of the Jordan River, watching in awe as the waters part before you, revealing a path to the promised land beyond. In that moment, there is a sense of wonder and anticipation, a recognition that change brings with it the promise of new beginnings and fresh opportunities. In the crucible of change, let faith be your anchor and courage your compass. For in embracing the unknown with open hearts and minds, you discover the richness and abundance that await on the other side of fear.

Prayer: Heavenly Father, grant us the courage to embrace change and the faith to trust in Your perfect plan for our lives. Help us to recognize the opportunities for growth and transformation that come with each new season, knowing that You are always at work, making all things new. Amen.

DAY 274
FINDING HOPE IN UNCERTAIN TIMES: TRUSTING IN A BRIGHTER FUTURE

Scripture Reference: Jeremiah 29:11 (KJV) "For I know the thoughts that I think toward you, saith the Lord, thoughts of peace, and not of evil, to give you an expected end."

In the crucible of uncertainty, find hope and assurance in the promise of God's faithfulness, dear warrior. For He knows the plans He has for you, plans to prosper you and not to harm you, plans to give you hope and a future. Imagine walking through the valley of the shadow of death, surrounded by darkness and uncertainty on every side. In that moment, there is a glimmer of light shining in the distance, a beacon of hope that pierces through the darkness and guides you safely home. In the crucible of uncertainty, let trust be your anchor and hope your guiding star. For in placing your faith in the hands of the One who holds the future, you discover the peace that surpasses all understanding and the assurance that His promises never fail.

Prayer: Lord, in uncertain times, grant us the strength to trust in Your faithfulness and the courage to hope in Your promises. Help us to fix our eyes on the bright future You have prepared for us, knowing that Your plans for us are good and filled with hope. Amen.

DAY 275
RESILIENCE IN LEADERSHIP: INSPIRING OTHERS THROUGH CHALLENGES

Scripture Reference: Joshua 1:9 (KJV) "Have not I commanded thee? Be strong and of a good courage; be not afraid, neither be thou dismayed: for the Lord thy God is with thee whithersoever thou goest."

In the crucible of leadership, cultivate resilience and courage, dear warrior. As God commanded Joshua, be strong and courageous, for the Lord your God is with you wherever you go, leading and guiding you through every challenge and trial. Imagine standing at the helm of a ship, navigating through stormy seas and treacherous waters. In that moment, there is a sense of purpose and determination, a recognition that true leadership is not measured by the absence of challenges but by the strength and courage to face them head-on. In the crucible of leadership, let integrity be your compass and humility your strength. For in leading by example and inspiring others through your actions, you create a legacy of resilience that transcends the trials of the present and paves the way for a brighter future.

Prayer: Heavenly Father, bless our leaders with resilience and courage, that they may inspire others through the challenges of life. Grant them the wisdom to lead with integrity and humility, trusting in Your guidance and provision every step of the way. Amen.

DAY 276
EMBRACING IMPERFECTION: FINDING BEAUTY IN THE FLAWS

Scripture Reference: 2 Corinthians 12:9 (KJV) "And he said unto me, My grace is sufficient for thee: for my strength is made perfect in weakness. Most gladly therefore will I rather glory in my infirmities, that the power of Christ may rest upon me."

In the crucible of imperfection, find beauty and grace in the flaws, dear warrior. For it is in our weaknesses that the power of Christ is made perfect, and His grace is sufficient to carry us through every trial and tribulation. Imagine standing before a mirror, gazing at your reflection with eyes of love and acceptance. In that moment, there is a sense of liberation and freedom, a recognition that true beauty lies not in perfection but in authenticity and vulnerability. In the crucible of imperfection, let compassion be your guide and forgiveness your practice. For in embracing your flaws and imperfections with humility and grace, you create space for healing and growth, allowing the power of Christ to rest upon you and transform your weaknesses into strengths.

Prayer: Lord, teach us to embrace our imperfections with humility and grace, knowing that Your strength is made perfect in our weakness. Help us to find beauty and grace in the flaws, trusting in Your sufficiency to carry us through every trial and tribulation. Amen.

DAY 277
THE STRENGTH OF UNITY: STANDING TOGETHER IN SOLIDARITY

Scripture Reference: Ecclesiastes 4:9-10 (KJV) "Two are better than one; because they have a good reward for their labour. For if they fall, the one will lift up his fellow: but woe to him that is alone when he falleth; for he hath not another to help him up."

In the crucible of unity, discover the strength and power that come from standing together in solidarity, dear warrior. As the writer of Ecclesiastes observes, two are better than one, for they can lift each other up in times of need and support one another through every trial and tribulation. Imagine linking arms with your brothers and sisters in Christ, standing shoulder to shoulder against the forces of darkness and division. In that moment, there is a sense of unity and purpose, a recognition that when we are united in heart and mind, nothing can stand against us. In the crucible of unity, let love be your bond and compassion your strength. For in coming together as one body, united in purpose and vision, we become a force to be reckoned with, bringing light and hope to a world in need of healing and reconciliation.

Prayer: Heavenly Father, unite us as one body, bound together by the bonds of love and compassion. Help us to stand together in solidarity, supporting and uplifting one another through every trial and tribulation, that Your light may shine brightly through us to the world. Amen.

DAY 278
FINDING JOY IN THE JOURNEY: CELEBRATING SMALL VICTORIES

Scripture Reference: Psalm 118:24 (KJV) "This is the day which the Lord hath made; we will rejoice and be glad in it."

In the crucible of life's journey, find joy and celebration in the small victories along the way, dear warrior. As the psalmist declares, "This is the day which the Lord has made; let us rejoice and be glad in it." Imagine dancing in the rain, feeling the rhythm of life pulsating through your veins and the warmth of God's love surrounding you like a blanket. In that moment, there is a sense of gratitude and wonder, a recognition that every day is a gift to be cherished and celebrated. In the crucible of life's journey, let gratitude be your song and joy your dance. For in rejoicing in the small victories and blessings that adorn our path, we discover the abundance and richness of life that can only be found in the presence of the Lord.

Prayer: Lord, help us to find joy and celebration in the small victories along life's journey, knowing that every day is a gift from You. Fill our hearts with gratitude and wonder, that we may rejoice and be glad in the precious moments You have given us. Amen.

DAY 279
OVERCOMING FEAR: STEPPING OUT OF COMFORT ZONES

Scripture Reference: 2 Timothy 1:7 (KJV) "For God hath not given us the spirit of fear; but of power, and of love, and of a sound mind."

In the crucible of fear, find courage and strength in the promises of God, dear warrior. For He has not given us a spirit of fear, but of power, love, and a sound mind, equipping us to overcome every obstacle and challenge that comes our way. Imagine standing at the edge of a cliff, peering over the edge into the unknown depths below.

In that moment, there is a choice to be made—to retreat in fear or to step forward in faith, trusting in the One who goes before us and makes a way where there seems to be no way. In the crucible of fear, let faith be your shield and courage your sword. For in stepping out of our comfort zones and facing our fears head-on, we discover the strength and resilience that can only be found in the presence of the Lord.

Prayer: Heavenly Father, grant us the courage to overcome our fears and step out of our comfort zones, trusting in Your promises and provision every step of the way. Fill us with Your power, love, and sound mind, that we may face every challenge with faith and confidence in You. Amen.

DAY 280
EMBRACING RESILIENCE: BOUNCING BACK STRONGER THAN BEFORE

Scripture Reference: Psalm 34:19 (KJV) "Many are the afflictions of the righteous: but the Lord delivereth him out of them all.",

In the crucible of resilience, discover the strength and courage that come from bouncing back stronger than before, dear warrior. As the psalmist proclaims, "Many are the afflictions of the righteous, but the Lord delivers him out of them all." Imagine standing in the aftermath of a storm, surveying the wreckage and devastation that surrounds you. In that moment, there is a choice to be made—to succumb to despair or to rise up with renewed determination, knowing that the Lord is with you and will deliver you from every trial and tribulation. In the crucible of resilience, let perseverance be your virtue and hope your anchor. For in bouncing back stronger than before, you discover the depth of your strength and the breadth of God's love, empowering you to overcome every obstacle that stands in your way.

Prayer: Lord, grant us the resilience to bounce back stronger than before, knowing that You are with us and will deliver us from every trial and tribulation. Help us to persevere in faith and hope, trusting in Your promises and provision to carry us through every storm. Amen.

DAY 281
THE POWER OF COMPASSION: EXTENDING KINDNESS IN TIMES OF NEED

Scripture Reference: Ephesians 4:32 (KJV) "And be ye kind one to another, tender-hearted, forgiving one another, even as God for Christ's sake hath forgiven you."

In the crucible of compassion, discover the transformative power of kindness and empathy, dear warrior. As the apostle Paul exhorts, be kind to one another, tender-hearted, forgiving each other as God in

Christ forgave you. Imagine walking through the streets of Jerusalem, witnessing the compassion of Jesus as He healed the sick, fed the hungry, and comforted the broken hearted. In His presence, there is a warmth and tenderness that melts away the hardness of hearts and brings healing to wounded souls. In the crucible of compassion, let love be your language and empathy your practice. For in extending kindness to those in need, you become a vessel of God's grace and a beacon of hope in a world that often feels dark and despairing.

Prayer: Heavenly Father, teach us to be kind and compassionate to one another, following the example of Your Son Jesus Christ. Fill our hearts with Your love and tender-heartedness, that we may extend kindness to those in need and be a source of comfort and healing in a hurting world. Amen.

DAY 282
CULTIVATING RESILIENT COMMUNITIES: SUPPORTING EACH OTHER THROUGH TOUGH TIMES

Scripture Reference: Galatians 6:2 (KJV) "Bear ye one another's burdens, and so fulfil the law of Christ."

In the crucible of community, cultivate resilience and strength by bearing one another's burdens, dear warrior. As the apostle Paul instructs, bear each other's burdens, thereby fulfilling the law of Christ. Imagine gathering with your brothers and sisters in faith, sharing each other's joys and sorrows, triumphs and tribulations. In that sacred space, there is a sense of unity and solidarity that binds hearts together and fortifies spirits against the storms of life. In the crucible of community, let compassion be your guide and generosity your practice. For in supporting and uplifting one another through tough times, you create a resilient and thriving community that reflects the love and grace of our Lord Jesus Christ.

Prayer: Lord, bless our communities with resilience and strength, that we may support and uplift one another through every trial and tribulation. Help us to bear each other's burdens with love and compassion, fulfilling the law of Christ and shining Your light to the world. Amen.

DAY 283
EMBRACING DIVERSITY: FINDING STRENGTH IN OUR DIFFERENCES

Scripture Reference: Romans 12:4-5 (KJV) "For as we have many members in one body, and all members have not the same office: So we, being many, are one body in Christ, and every one members one of another."

In the crucible of diversity, discover the beauty and strength that come from embracing our differences, dear warrior. As the apostle

Paul writes, we are many members in one body, each with unique gifts and talents, yet all belonging to Christ and to one another. Imagine standing in the midst of a diverse and vibrant community, where people of different backgrounds, cultures, and experiences come together as one family in Christ. In that sacred space, there is a richness and depth that transcends our differences and unites us in love and fellowship. In the crucible of diversity, let acceptance be your posture and unity your goal. For in celebrating our differences and embracing the unique contributions of each member, we become a more vibrant and resilient body of Christ, reflecting the diversity and beauty of God's creation.

Prayer: Heavenly Father, help us to embrace diversity and celebrate our differences, knowing that we are all one body in Christ. Fill our hearts with love and acceptance for one another, that we may build a community that reflects Your kingdom here on earth. Amen.

DAY 284
FINDING PURPOSE IN PAIN: TRANSFORMING SUFFERING INTO GROWTH

Scripture Reference: Romans 8:28 (KJV) "And we know that all things work together for good to them that love God, to them who are the called according to his purpose.",

In the crucible of pain, discover the purpose and meaning that come from trusting in God's plan, dear warrior. As the apostle Paul assures us, all things work together for good to those who love God and are called according to His purpose. Imagine standing at the foot of the cross, witnessing the agony and suffering of Jesus as He bore the weight of our sins upon His shoulders. In that moment of darkness and despair, there is a glimmer of hope and redemption, a recognition that even in our deepest pain, God is at work, bringing beauty from ashes and joy from mourning. In the crucible of pain, let faith be your anchor and hope your refuge. For in entrusting your suffering to the hands of a loving and sovereign God, you discover the transformative power of grace and the promise of a future filled with hope and purpose.

Prayer: Lord, in times of pain and suffering, grant us the faith to trust in Your plan and the hope to see Your purpose at work in our lives. Help us to find meaning and growth in our struggles, knowing that You are with us and working all things together for our good. Amen.

DAY 285

RESILIENCE IN THE STORM: WEATHERING LIFE'S CHALLENGES WITH GRACE

Scripture Reference: Psalm 46:1-3 (KJV) "God is our refuge and strength, a very present help in trouble. Therefore, will not we fear, though the earth be removed, and though the mountains be carried into the midst of the sea; Though the waters thereof roar and be troubled, though the mountains shake with the swelling thereof."

In the crucible of the storm, find refuge and strength in the presence of God, dear warrior. As the psalmist declares, God is our refuge and strength, a very present help in trouble, therefore we will not fear, though the earth be removed and the mountains be carried into the midst of the sea. Imagine standing on the shore of a raging sea, feeling the wind howling and the waves crashing around you. In that moment of chaos and turmoil, there is a peace that surpasses all understanding, a recognition that God is with you, guiding you safely through the storm. In the crucible of the storm, let faith be your anchor and trust your shield. For in weathering life's challenges with grace and courage, you discover the resilience and strength that can only be found in the presence of the Lord.

Prayer: Heavenly Father, be our refuge and strength in the midst of life's storms, guiding us safely through every trial and tribulation. Help us to trust in Your presence and to find peace in the midst of chaos, knowing that You are with us and will never leave us nor forsake us. Amen.

DAY 286

EMBRACING CHANGE: EMBRACING OPPORTUNITIES FOR TRANSFORMATION

Scripture Reference: Isaiah 43:19 (KJV) "Behold, I will do a new thing; now it shall spring forth; shall ye not know it? I will even make a way in the wilderness, and rivers in the desert."

In the crucible of change, embrace the opportunities for transformation and growth, dear warrior. As the prophet Isaiah proclaims, God is constantly doing a new thing, making a way in the wilderness and rivers in the desert of our lives. Imagine standing on the threshold of a new beginning, feeling the excitement and anticipation of what lies ahead. In that moment of uncertainty and possibility, there is a sense of wonder and adventure, a recognition that change brings with it the promise of new opportunities and blessings. In the crucible of change, let faith be your guide and courage your companion. For in embracing the unknown with open hearts and minds, you discover the richness and abundance that await on the other side of fear.

Prayer: Lord, grant us the courage to embrace change and the faith to trust in Your perfect plan for our lives. Help us to recognize the opportunities for transformation and growth that come with each new

season, knowing that You are always at work, making all things new.
Amen.

DAY 287
THE POWER OF RESILIENCE: THRIVING IN THE FACE OF ADVERSITY

Scripture Reference: James 1:2-4 (KJV) "My brethren, count it all joy when ye fall into divers temptations; Knowing this, that the trying of your faith worketh patience. But let patience have her perfect work, that ye may be perfect and entire, wanting nothing."

In the crucible of adversity, discover the power and strength that come from resilience, dear warrior. As the apostle James teaches, count it all joy when you face trials of various kinds, for the testing of your faith produces perseverance, and let perseverance finish its work so that you may be mature and complete, lacking in nothing. Imagine standing in the midst of a fiery trial, feeling the heat and pressure bearing down upon you.

In that moment of testing and refinement, there is a resilience that rises up within you, a determination to press on and overcome every obstacle that stands in your way. In the crucible of adversity, let joy be your song and perseverance your anthem. For in facing life's challenges with courage and grace, you discover the depth of your strength and the breadth of God's love, empowering you to thrive in the face of adversity.

Prayer: Heavenly Father, grant us the resilience to thrive in the face of adversity, knowing that You are with us and will never leave us nor forsake us. Help us to count it all joy when we face trials of various kinds, knowing that the testing of our faith produces perseverance and maturity in You. Amen.

DAY 288
FINDING LIGHT IN DARKNESS: CULTIVATING HOPE IN DIFFICULT TIMES

Scripture Reference: Psalm 119:105 (KJV) "Thy word is a lamp unto my feet, and a light unto my path."

In the crucible of darkness, find hope and illumination in the Word of God, dear warrior. As the psalmist declares, God's word is a lamp unto our feet and a light unto our path, guiding us through the darkest of times and leading us into the brightness of His presence. Imagine walking through a dense forest at night, feeling the weight of darkness pressing in around you. In that moment of uncertainty and fear, there is a flicker of light shining in the distance, a beacon of hope that leads you safely home. In the crucible of darkness, let faith be your guide and hope your anchor. For in clinging to the promises of God and His unfailing love, you discover the strength and courage to face every trial and tribulation with confidence and grace.

Prayer: Lord, be our light in the darkness, guiding us through every trial and tribulation with Your unfailing love and grace. Help us to trust in Your promises and to find hope in Your presence, knowing that You are with us always, leading us into the brightness of Your eternal light. Amen.

DAY 289
OVERCOMING OBSTACLES: BREAKING THROUGH BARRIERS TO SUCCESS

Scripture Reference: Philippians 4:13 (KJV) "I can do all things through Christ which strengthened me."

In the crucible of obstacles, discover the strength and power that come from Christ, dear warrior. As the apostle Paul declares, I can do all things through Christ who strengthens me, empowering us to overcome every barrier and obstacle that stands in our way. Imagine standing at the foot of a towering mountain, feeling the weight of doubt and fear pressing in around you. In that moment of uncertainty and hesitation, there is a voice that whispers in your ear, reminding you of the One who goes before you, making a way where there seems to be no way. In the crucible of obstacles, let faith be your courage and determination your resolve. For in trusting in the strength and power of Christ within you, you discover the resilience and tenacity to press on and achieve the impossible.

Prayer: Heavenly Father, strengthen us to overcome every obstacle and barrier that stands in our way, knowing that we can do all things through Christ who strengthens us. Help us to trust in Your provision and guidance, knowing that You are with us always, leading us to victory. Amen.

DAY 290
EMBRACING RESILIENCE: BUILDING INNER STRENGTH AND FORTITUDE

Scripture Reference: 1 Corinthians 16:13 (KJV) "Watch ye, stand fast in the faith, quit you like men, be strong."

In the crucible of resilience, build inner strength and fortitude by standing firm in the faith, dear warrior. As the apostle Paul exhorts, watch, stand fast in the faith, be brave, be strong. Imagine standing on the battlefield of life, feeling the winds of adversity blowing all around you. In that moment of testing and trial, there is a resolve that rises up within you, a determination to stand firm and not be shaken by the storms that rage. In the crucible of resilience, let faith be your foundation and courage your armor. For in trusting in the promises of God and His unwavering love, you discover the strength and fortitude to face every challenge with grace and confidence.

Prayer: Lord, help us to embrace resilience and build inner strength and fortitude by standing firm in the faith. Fill us with Your courage and strength, that we may face every trial and tribulation with confidence and grace, knowing that You are with us always. Amen.

DAY 291
THE POWER OF RESILIENT FAITH: TRUSTING IN GOD'S PLAN

Scripture: "Trust in the Lord with all thine heart; and lean not unto thine own understanding. In all thy ways acknowledge him, and he shall direct thy paths." - Proverbs 3:5-6 (KJV)

In the tumultuous journey of life, your faith serves as an anchor amidst the stormy seas. Resilient faith doesn't falter in the face of uncertainty; it flourishes, knowing that God's plan is perfect. Just as a soldier trusts in their commander's strategy, so too must you trust in the divine plan laid out before you. Though you may not comprehend every twist and turn, rest assured that every step is ordered by the Almighty. In moments of doubt, recall the promises of scripture. Remember the countless times God has delivered you from adversity. Let your faith be your shield, protecting you from the arrows of fear and doubt. Surrender your worries and anxieties to the One who holds the universe in His hands.

Prayer: Heavenly Father, grant me unwavering faith to trust in Your divine plan, even when the path ahead seems uncertain. Help me to lean not on my own understanding but to acknowledge Your wisdom in all things. In Jesus' name, amen.

DAY 292

CULTIVATING RESILIENT MINDS: NURTURING MENTAL HEALTH AND WELL-BEING

Scripture: "And be not conformed to this world: but be ye transformed by the renewing of your mind, that ye may prove what is that good, and acceptable, and perfect, will of God." - Romans 12:2 (KJV)

Just as physical training is essential for military readiness, so too is the cultivation of a resilient mind crucial for navigating life's challenges. Your mental well-being is a precious asset, requiring diligent care and nurturing. Fill your mind with thoughts that uplift and inspire, guarding against the negativity that seeks to infiltrate. In the barracks of your mind, let the truths of Scripture stand as sentinels, guarding against the enemy's onslaught of doubt and despair. Engage in practices that promote mental health, such as meditation, prayer, and seeking professional help when needed. Remember, it is not a sign of weakness to seek assistance but a testament to your strength and courage.

Prayer: Gracious God, grant me the wisdom to prioritize my mental health and well-being. Help me to guard my thoughts diligently and to nurture a resilient mind that is anchored in Your truth. Strengthen me to seek help when needed and to support others in their journey towards wholeness. In Jesus' name, amen.

DAY 293
EMBRACING VULNERABILITY: FINDING STRENGTH IN OPENNESS

Scripture: "But he said to me, 'My grace is sufficient for you, for my power is made perfect in weakness.' Therefore, I will boast all the more gladly about my weaknesses, so that Christ's power may rest on me." - 2 Corinthians 12:9 (KJV)

In a world that often values stoicism and self-reliance, embracing vulnerability may seem counterintuitive. Yet, it is through our weaknesses that God's strength is made perfect. By allowing ourselves to be vulnerable, we invite His grace to work powerfully within us. Do not fear vulnerability, for it is not a sign of weakness but of authenticity and courage. Share your struggles with trusted comrades and lean on the support of your faith community. In vulnerability, you will find strength, for it is in acknowledging our limitations that we open ourselves to divine intervention.

Prayer: Heavenly Father, grant me the courage to embrace vulnerability and to find strength in openness. Help me to trust in Your grace, knowing that Your power is made perfect in my weaknesses. May I be a beacon of hope to others as I share my journey authentically. In Jesus' name, amen.

DAY 294

FINDING PEACE IN THE PRESENT: LETTING GO OF PAST REGRETS

Scripture: "Brethren, I count not myself to have apprehended: but this one thing I do, forgetting those things which are behind, and reaching forth unto those things which are before, I press toward the mark for the prize of the high calling of God in Christ Jesus." - Philippians 3:13-14 (KJV)

Regrets from the past can weigh heavily on the soul, hindering your ability to fully embrace the present. But remember, in Christ, you are a new creation, and His grace offers freedom from the burdens of yesterday. Let go of past mistakes and failures, for dwelling on them only serves to rob you of the joy and peace found in the present moment. Instead, fix your gaze on the hope-filled future that awaits you. Trust in God's redemptive power to turn even the darkest moments of your past into opportunities for growth and transformation.

Prayer: Gracious God, grant me the strength to release the weight of past regrets and to embrace the abundant life You have called me to live. Help me to focus on the present moment, trusting in Your grace to guide me forward. May Your redemption be evident in every area of my life. In Jesus' name, amen.

DAY 295
RESILIENCE IN RELATIONSHIPS: BUILDING
TRUST AND CONNECTION

Scripture: "Above all, love each other deeply, because love covers over a multitude of sins." - 1 Peter 4:8 (KJV)

Strong relationships are built on a foundation of trust, communication, and genuine love. Just as soldiers rely on their comrades for support in the heat of battle, so too must you cultivate resilient relationships with those around you. Invest time and effort into nurturing meaningful connections with your fellow soldiers, friends, and family members. Practice active listening, empathy, and forgiveness, knowing that love covers a multitude of sins. Build each other up, offering support and encouragement in both times of triumph and trial.

Prayer: Loving Father, teach me to love others deeply and authentically, just as You have loved me. Help me to cultivate resilient relationships built on trust, communication, and mutual respect. May Your love flow through me, strengthening the bonds of connection with those around me. In Jesus' name, amen.

DAY 296
EMBRACING CHANGE: EMBRACING THE SEASONS OF LIFE

Scripture: "To everything there is a season, and a time to every purpose under the heaven." - Ecclesiastes 3:1 (KJV)

Change is inevitable in life, just as the seasons change with the passing of time. Embrace the ebb and flow of life's transitions, trusting that each season serves a purpose ordained by God. Whether you find yourself in a season of abundance or scarcity, joy or sorrow, know that He is with you every step of the way. Adaptability is a hallmark of resilience, allowing you to navigate the shifting tides with grace and courage. Embrace change as an opportunity for growth and renewal, knowing that God is orchestrating all things for your ultimate good. Surrender your plans to His perfect will, confident that He who holds the future is faithful.

Prayer: Sovereign Lord, grant me the wisdom to embrace change as a natural part of life's journey. Help me to trust in Your timing and purpose, even when the path ahead is uncertain. May I find strength and courage in knowing that You are with me in every season. In Jesus' name, amen.

DAY 297

THE POWER OF PERSEVERANCE: STAYING STRONG IN THE FACE OF CHALLENGES

Scripture: "And let us not be weary in well doing: for in due season we shall reap, if we faint not." - Galatians 6:9 (KJV)

In the midst of life's trials and tribulations, perseverance becomes your greatest ally. Like a soldier pressing forward despite the obstacles, persevere in doing good, knowing that your labour is not in vain. Though the journey may be fraught with challenges, do not grow weary, for a harvest of blessings awaits those who endure. Draw strength from the examples of perseverance found throughout Scripture, from the endurance of Job to the steadfastness of Paul. Fix your eyes on the prize set before you, trusting in the faithfulness of God to sustain you through every trial. Stand firm in your resolve, knowing that victory belongs to those who persevere to the end.

Prayer: Almighty God, grant me the strength to persevere in the face of adversity, knowing that You are my ever-present help in times of trouble. Strengthen my resolve to press on, even when the path ahead seems daunting. May I find courage and endurance in Your promises, knowing that You are faithful to fulfill them. In Jesus' name, amen.

DAY 298

CULTIVATING RESILIENT HEARTS: FOSTERING COMPASSION AND EMPATHY

Scripture: "Finally, be ye all of one mind, having compassion one of another, love as brethren, be pitiful, be courteous." - 1 Peter 3:8 (KJV)

Resilience extends beyond personal fortitude; it encompasses the capacity to empathize and connect with others in their struggles. Cultivate a heart of compassion, mirroring the love and empathy demonstrated by Christ himself. Treat others with kindness and understanding, recognizing that everyone is fighting battles known only to them. Take the time to truly listen to the stories of those around you, offering a shoulder to lean on and a listening ear to hear their concerns. Practice empathy in your interactions, seeking to understand the perspective of others without judgment. In doing so, you will not only strengthen your own resilience but also foster unity and camaraderie within your community.

Prayer: Compassionate Father, open my heart to the needs of those around me, that I may show kindness and empathy to all. Help me to be a source of comfort and support to those who are struggling, offering love and understanding in abundance. May Your compassion flow through me, touching lives and bringing healing to broken hearts. In Jesus' name, amen.

DAY 299

EMBRACING GRATITUDE: FINDING JOY IN EVERYDAY BLESSINGS

Scripture: "In everything give thanks: for this is the will of God in Christ Jesus concerning you." - 1 Thessalonians 5:18 (KJV)

Gratitude is a powerful antidote to despair, shifting your focus from what you lack to the abundance that surrounds you. Even in the midst of life's challenges, cultivate a spirit of thanksgiving, acknowledging the countless blessings bestowed upon you each day. Pause to reflect on the simple joys that enrich your life, from the warmth of the sun on your face to the laughter of loved ones gathered around you. Train your heart to find gratitude in all circumstances, knowing that even the trials you face serve a purpose in God's greater plan.

Prayer: Gracious God, teach me to cultivate a heart of gratitude, that I may find joy in every blessing You bestow upon me. Help me to recognize Your goodness in both the triumphs and trials of life, trusting that Your hand is ever at work for my ultimate good. May thanksgiving overflow from my heart, as I give praise to You in all things. In Jesus' name, amen.

DAY 300

CELEBRATING MILESTONES: REFLECTING ON GROWTH AND ACHIEVEMENT

Scripture: "Blessed be the Lord God of Israel from everlasting to everlasting: and let all the people say, Amen. Praise ye the Lord." - Psalm 106:48 (KJV)

As you reach this significant milestone, take a moment to pause and reflect on the journey that has brought you to this point. Celebrate the growth and achievements that have marked your path, giving thanks to the Lord who has sustained you through every trial and triumph. Remember that every milestone is an opportunity to acknowledge God's faithfulness and goodness in your life. Whether large or small, each accomplishment is a testament to His grace and provision. Look ahead with hope and anticipation, knowing that the best is yet to come as you continue to walk in obedience to His will.

Prayer: Heavenly Father, I praise You for bringing me to this significant milestone in my journey. Thank You for Your faithfulness and provision every step of the way. As I reflect on the growth and achievements of the past, I look forward with hope and anticipation to the future You have prepared for me. May all honor and glory be Yours, now and forevermore. In Jesus' name, amen.

DAY 301
RESILIENCE IN THE JOURNEY: NAVIGATING
LIFE'S TWISTS AND TURNS

Scripture: "Trust in the Lord with all thine heart; and lean not unto thine own understanding. In all thy ways acknowledge him, and he shall direct thy paths." - Proverbs 3:5-6 (KJV)

Life is a journey filled with unexpected twists and turns, but your faith in God provides a steadfast anchor amidst the storms. Trust in His guidance, knowing that He will direct your path even when the way forward seems uncertain. Just as the Israelites followed the pillar of cloud by day and the pillar of fire by night, so too must you follow the leading of the Holy Spirit in your journey. Though the road may be rocky and the path may be steep, take heart in the promise that God is with you every step of the way. Lean not on your own understanding, but acknowledge His sovereignty over your life. In His hands, even the most challenging detours can lead to unexpected blessings.

Prayer: Heavenly Father, as I navigate life's twists and turns, I place my trust in You to guide me. Give me the wisdom to follow Your leading and the faith to trust in Your plan, even when it leads me down unfamiliar paths. May Your presence be my constant companion on this journey. In Jesus' name, amen.

DAY 302
EMBRACING RESILIENCE: HARNESSING STRENGTH IN ADVERSITY

Scripture: "I can do all things through Christ which strengthened me." - Philippians 4:13 (KJV)

In the face of adversity, you possess a reservoir of strength that transcends your own abilities. Draw upon the power of Christ within you, knowing that His strength is made perfect in your weakness. Just as a soldier is fortified by rigorous training, so too are you equipped to overcome any obstacle that comes your way. Embrace resilience as a spiritual discipline, honing your ability to persevere in the midst of trials. Refuse to be overcome by despair, for you are more than a conqueror through Him who loves you. Trust in the promise that God works all things together for your good, even the trials that threaten to overwhelm you.

Prayer: Gracious God, grant me the courage to face adversity with resilience, knowing that Your strength sustains me. Help me to draw upon the power of Christ within me, finding hope and perseverance in the midst of life's challenges. May Your grace be my strength in times of weakness. In Jesus' name, amen.

DAY 303
THE POWER OF CONNECTION: BUILDING SUPPORTIVE RELATIONSHIPS

Scripture: "Two are better than one; because they have a good reward for their labour. For if they fall, the one will lift up his fellow: but woe to him that is alone when he falleth; for he hath not another to help him up." - Ecclesiastes 4:9-10 (KJV)

In the journey of life, companionship is a precious gift from God. Cultivate supportive relationships with fellow believers, for they provide strength and encouragement in times of need. Just as iron sharpens iron, so too do faithful friends sharpen one another. Be intentional about fostering connections with those who share your faith and values. Surround yourself with individuals who will lift you up when you stumble and rejoice with you in times of triumph. Together, you can weather the storms of life and celebrate the joys of fellowship.

Prayer: Heavenly Father, thank You for the gift of supportive relationships that You have placed in my life. Help me to cultivate deep connections with fellow believers, that we may strengthen and encourage one another in our faith. May our bonds of friendship be a reflection of Your love and grace. In Jesus' name, amen.

DAY 304

FINDING PURPOSE IN PAIN: TURNING CHALLENGES INTO OPPORTUNITIES

Scripture: "And we know that all things work together for good to them that love God, to them who are the called according to his purpose." - Romans 8:28 (KJV)

Even in the midst of pain and suffering, God is at work, weaving a tapestry of redemption and purpose. Trust in His promise that all things, even the most difficult trials, work together for your ultimate good. Just as Joseph's suffering ultimately led to the salvation of his family, so too can your pain be transformed into a testimony of God's faithfulness. Seek God's purpose in the midst of your pain, knowing that He wastes nothing in His economy of grace. Allow your struggles to deepen your reliance on Him and to refine your character, shaping you into the image of Christ. In the hands of the Master Potter, even brokenness can be molded into beauty.

Prayer: Sovereign Lord, grant me the faith to see Your hand at work in the midst of my pain. Help me to trust in Your promise that all things work together for my good and Your glory. Give me the courage to embrace the purpose You have for me, even when it is born out of hardship. In Jesus' name, amen.

DAY 305

RESILIENCE IN ACTION: TAKING STEPS TOWARDS PERSONAL GROWTH

Scripture: "But grow in grace, and in the knowledge of our Lord and Saviour Jesus Christ. To him be glory both now and for ever. Amen." - 2 Peter 3:18 (KJV)

Resilience is not merely about weathering the storms of life but also about actively pursuing personal growth and development. Just as a seed must push through the soil to reach the sunlight, so too must you take intentional steps towards spiritual maturity. Commit yourself to a lifelong journey of growth in grace and knowledge of Christ. Cultivate spiritual disciplines such as prayer, Bible study, and fellowship with other believers. Allow the challenges you face to refine your character and deepen your faith, trusting that God is at work in every season of life.

Prayer: Gracious God, help me to embrace resilience as an active pursuit of personal growth and spiritual maturity. Grant me the discipline to cultivate a deeper relationship with You and the courage to face the challenges that come my way. May my life be a reflection of Your grace and glory. In Jesus' name, amen.

DAY 306
EMBRACING CHANGE: EMBRACING NEW BEGINNINGS

Scripture: "Behold, I will do a new thing; now it shall spring forth; shall ye not know it? I will even make a way in the wilderness, and rivers in the desert." - Isaiah 43:19 (KJV)

Change can be unsettling, but it also offers the opportunity for growth and renewal. Just as the Israelites experienced God's faithfulness as they journeyed through the wilderness, so too can you trust in His promise to make a way in the midst of change. Embrace new beginnings with faith and anticipation, knowing that God is orchestrating all things for your good. Release the grip of fear and uncertainty, and step boldly into the unknown, confident that the Lord goes before you to pave the way.

Prayer: Heavenly Father, as I face new beginnings and changes in my life, grant me the courage to embrace them with faith and trust in Your unfailing love. Help me to see Your hand at work in every season of change, knowing that You are making all things new. May I walk in step with Your purposes, confident in Your provision and guidance. In Jesus' name, amen.

DAY 307
CULTIVATING RESILIENT SPIRITS: NURTURING INNER STRENGTH

Scripture: "But they that wait upon the Lord shall renew their strength; they shall mount up with wings as eagles; they shall run, and not be weary; and they shall walk, and not faint." - Isaiah 40:31 (KJV)

Resilience begins within the depths of your spirit, where faith takes root and strength is nourished. Like a well-tended garden, cultivate a resilient spirit by immersing yourself in the presence of the Lord and drawing strength from His Word. In moments of weariness and doubt, wait upon the Lord, for He promises to renew your strength. Surrender your burdens to Him and allow His Spirit to breathe new life into your weary soul. As you abide in Him, you will find the strength to soar on wings like eagles, to run with endurance, and to walk in unwavering faith.

Prayer: Gracious God, I thank You for the promise of renewed strength for those who wait upon You. Fill me with Your Spirit and nourish my spirit with Your Word, that I may cultivate resilience from within. Help me to lean on You in times of weakness and find strength in Your presence. In Jesus' name, amen.

DAY 308

THE POWER OF RESILIENT HOPE: HOLDING ONTO FAITH IN DIFFICULT TIMES

Scripture: "Now the God of hope fill you with all joy and peace in believing, that ye may abound in hope, through the power of the Holy Ghost." - Romans 15:13 (KJV)

In the darkest of times, resilient hope shines as a beacon of light, guiding you through the storm. Anchor your faith in the promises of God, for He is the source of all hope and the giver of peace that surpasses understanding. Though the winds may howl and the waves may rage, cling to the hope that is found in Christ Jesus. Let your faith be an unshakable foundation, standing firm against the onslaught of doubt and despair. As you trust in the power of the Holy Spirit, you will abound in hope, overflowing with joy and peace that transcends circumstances.

Prayer: Heavenly Father, in times of difficulty and uncertainty, I turn to You as the source of my hope and strength. Fill me with Your joy and peace as I place my trust in Your promises. Help me to hold onto resilient hope, knowing that You are faithful to fulfill Your purposes. In Jesus' name, amen.

DAY 309
EMBRACING GRATITUDE: FINDING BEAUTY IN EVERYDAY MOMENTS

Scripture: "O give thanks unto the Lord; for he is good: for his mercy endureth for ever." - Psalm 136:1 (KJV)

Gratitude is a powerful force that can transform even the most ordinary moments into occasions for praise and thanksgiving. Cultivate a heart of gratitude by intentionally seeking out the beauty and blessings that surround you each day. Take time to pause and reflect on the goodness of the Lord, for His mercy endures forever. Even in the midst of trials and challenges, there is much to be thankful for. Train your heart to find joy in the simple pleasures of life, knowing that every good and perfect gift comes from above.

Prayer: Gracious God, I thank You for the countless blessings You have bestowed upon me, both big and small. Help me to cultivate a heart of gratitude, that I may find beauty in every moment and praise You for Your goodness. May my life be a testament to Your faithfulness and grace. In Jesus' name, amen.

DAY 310
RESILIENCE IN COMMUNITY: COMING TOGETHER IN TIMES OF NEED

Scripture: "Bear ye one another's burdens, and so fulfil the law of Christ." - Galatians 6:2 (KJV)

Resilience is not solely an individual endeavor but a collective journey shared within the community of believers. As members of the body of Christ, we are called to support and uplift one another, bearing each other's burdens in times of need. In times of trial and hardship, lean on your brothers and sisters in Christ for encouragement and support. Allow yourself to be vulnerable, knowing that you are surrounded by a community of love and compassion. Together, you can weather the storms of life and emerge stronger than before.

Prayer: Loving Father, thank You for the gift of community, where we can find support and encouragement in times of need. Help us to bear one another's burdens and to fulfill the law of Christ by loving one another deeply. May our unity be a reflection of Your love and grace to the world. In Jesus' name, amen.

DAY 311
EMBRACING VULNERABILITY: BUILDING AUTHENTIC CONNECTIONS

Scripture: "Confess your faults one to another, and pray one for another, that ye may be healed. The effectual fervent prayer of a righteous man availeth much." - James 5:16 (KJV)

True connection flourishes in the soil of vulnerability, where hearts are laid bare and authenticity reigns supreme. Just as Jesus openly shared His heart with His disciples, so too are you called to build genuine connections by being transparent and vulnerable with one another. Do not fear revealing your weaknesses and struggles, for in doing so, you create space for others to do the same. Through mutual vulnerability, you can offer support, encouragement, and prayers for one another's healing and growth.

Prayer: Gracious God, help me to embrace vulnerability as a pathway to authentic connections with others. Give me the courage to share my heart openly and to receive others with compassion and grace. May our relationships be strengthened as we bear each other's burdens and lift one another up in prayer. In Jesus' name, amen.

DAY 312
THE STRENGTH OF RESILIENT HEARTS:
OVERCOMING ADVERSITY WITH LOVE

Scripture: "And now abideth faith, hope, charity, these three; but the greatest of these is charity." - 1 Corinthians 13:13 (KJV)

Resilient hearts are fortified by love, the greatest of virtues. In the face of adversity, let love be your guiding light, for it has the power to conquer even the greatest challenges. Just as Christ's love knows no bounds, so too must you extend love to others, even in the midst of difficulty. Choose to respond to adversity with kindness, compassion, and forgiveness, knowing that love covers a multitude of sins. Through acts of love, you can overcome bitterness and resentment, fostering healing and reconciliation in your relationships.

Prayer: Heavenly Father, fill my heart with Your love, that I may overcome adversity with grace and compassion. Help me to extend love to others, even in the midst of trials, knowing that Your love never fails. May Your love shine brightly through me, bringing healing and reconciliation to those around me. In Jesus' name, amen.

DAY 313

FINDING BALANCE IN CHAOS: NAVIGATING LIFE'S CHALLENGES WITH GRACE

Scripture: "Be careful for nothing; but in everything by prayer and supplication with thanksgiving let your requests be made known unto God." - Philippians 4:6 (KJV)

In the chaos of life's challenges, find your anchor in prayer and gratitude. Just as Jesus calmed the stormy sea with a word, so too can you find peace in the midst of life's storms through prayerful surrender to God. Seek balance in all areas of your life, trusting in God's provision and guidance. Lean not on your own understanding, but acknowledge His sovereignty over every situation. With a heart full of thanksgiving, approach God with your requests, confident that He hears and answers the prayers of His children.

Prayer: Gracious God, in the midst of life's chaos, I turn to You as my source of peace and stability. Help me to find balance in every area of my life, trusting in Your provision and guidance. May my prayers be filled with thanksgiving, knowing that You are faithful to hear and answer. In Jesus' name, amen.

DAY 314
RESILIENCE IN THE UNKNOWN: TRUSTING IN THE JOURNEY AHEAD

Scripture: "Trust in the Lord with all thine heart; and lean not unto thine own understanding. In all thy ways acknowledge him, and he shall direct thy paths." - Proverbs 3:5-6 (KJV)

As you journey into the unknown, place your trust fully in the Lord, for He alone knows the path ahead. Though uncertainty may loom on the horizon, rest assured that God is faithful to guide and provide for His children. Let go of the need to control every outcome, and instead, surrender your plans and desires to God's perfect will. With each step you take, acknowledge His sovereignty and trust that He is working all things together for your good.

Prayer: Heavenly Father, as I venture into the unknown, I place my trust in You to guide and direct my path. Help me to lean not on my own understanding but to acknowledge Your wisdom in all things. Grant me the faith to trust in Your plan, even when the way forward seems unclear. In Jesus' name, amen.

DAY 315
EMBRACING CHANGE: FINDING STRENGTH IN ADAPTABILITY

Scripture: "For I am the Lord, I change not." - Malachi 3:6 (KJV)

In a world of constant change, find your stability in the unchanging nature of God. Though circumstances may shift and seasons may come and go, He remains steadfast and faithful through it all. Embrace change as an opportunity for growth and transformation, knowing that God works all things together for your good. Just as a tree bends and sways with the wind, so too must you adapt to the changes of life, trusting that God is with you every step of the way.

Prayer: Gracious God, in a world of constant change, I find my stability in Your unchanging nature. Help me to embrace change as an opportunity for growth and transformation, knowing that You are with me through every season of life. Grant me the strength to adapt and thrive in the midst of change. In Jesus' name, amen.

DAY 316
CULTIVATING RESILIENT MINDS: FOSTERING MENTAL WELL-BEING

Scripture: "And be not conformed to this world: but be ye transformed by the renewing of your mind, that ye may prove what is that good, and acceptable, and perfect, will of God." - Romans 12:2 (KJV)

Your mental well-being is a precious gift from God, deserving of careful attention and nurturing. Just as a garden requires tending to flourish, so too must you cultivate a resilient mind through the renewing of your thoughts. Guard your mind against the negative influences of the world, filling it instead with thoughts that are true, noble, pure, and praiseworthy. Engage in practices that promote mental health, such as prayer, meditation, and self-care. Trust in God's promise to renew your mind and lead you in His perfect will.

Prayer: Heavenly Father, I commit my mind to Your care, knowing that mental well-being is a gift from You. Help me to guard my thoughts diligently and to fill my mind with things that are pleasing to You. Grant me the strength to renew my mind daily through prayer and meditation on Your Word. In Jesus' name, amen.

DAY 317
THE POWER OF RESILIENT FAITH: TRUSTING IN DIVINE GUIDANCE

Scripture: "Thy word is a lamp unto my feet, and a light unto my path." - Psalm 119:105 (KJV)

In times of uncertainty, let the Word of God be your guiding light, illuminating the path before you. Just as the Israelites followed the pillar of cloud by day and the pillar of fire by night, so too can you trust in God's guidance through His Word and Spirit. Anchor your faith in the promises of Scripture, knowing that God is faithful to lead and direct your steps. As you seek His guidance in prayer and meditation on His Word, He will make your path clear and straight.

Prayer: Gracious God, thank You for the gift of Your Word, which serves as a lamp unto my feet and a light unto my path. Help me to trust in Your divine guidance, knowing that You are faithful to lead me in the way I should go. Grant me the wisdom to discern Your voice and the courage to follow where You lead. In Jesus' name, amen.

DAY 318

EMBRACING RESILIENCE: RISING STRONGER AFTER SETBACKS

Scripture: "But they that wait upon the Lord shall renew their strength; they shall mount up with wings as eagles; they shall run, and not be weary; and they shall walk, and not faint." - Isaiah 40:31 (KJV)

Setbacks are not the end of the road but an opportunity for a comeback. Just as the eagle rises stronger after each storm, so too can you soar above your setbacks with renewed strength from the Lord.

Wait upon the Lord in times of adversity, trusting in His promise to renew your strength. Though you may stumble and fall, He will lift you up and set you on high. With His help, you can overcome every obstacle and emerge victorious.

Prayer: Heavenly Father, thank You for the promise of renewed strength for those who wait upon You. Help me to rise stronger after setbacks, trusting in Your unfailing love and grace. Grant me the courage to press on, knowing that You are with me every step of the way. In Jesus' name, amen.

DAY 319
RESILIENCE IN RELATIONSHIPS: BUILDING STRONG BONDS THROUGH TRIALS

Scripture: "A friend loveth at all times, and a brother is born for adversity." - Proverbs 17:17 (KJV)

True friendships are forged in the fires of adversity, standing the test of time and trials. Just as Jonathan supported David in his darkest hours, so too must you cultivate relationships built on love, loyalty, and mutual support. Lean on your friends and loved ones in times of need, and be there for them in their hour of trial. Through shared experiences and heartfelt conversations, you can strengthen your bonds and weather life's storms together.

Prayer: Gracious God, thank You for the gift of friendships that stand the test of time and trials. Help me to be a loyal and supportive friend, offering love and encouragement to those in need. Grant me the wisdom to cultivate relationships built on mutual trust and respect. In Jesus' name, amen.

DAY 320
EMBRACING GRATITUDE: CULTIVATING THANKFULNESS IN ALL CIRCUMSTANCES

Scripture: "In everything give thanks: for this is the will of God in Christ Jesus concerning you." - 1 Thessalonians 5:18 (KJV)

Gratitude is a powerful antidote to despair, transforming even the darkest moments into opportunities for praise and thanksgiving. Just as Paul and Silas praised God in the midst of their imprisonment, so too can you cultivate a heart of gratitude in all circumstances. Find reasons to give thanks in every situation, knowing that God is at work for your good. Even in the midst of trials and difficulties, there is much to be thankful for. Choose to focus on the blessings rather than the burdens, and watch as gratitude transforms your outlook on life.

Prayer: Heavenly Father, help me to cultivate a heart of gratitude, knowing that You are the source of every good and perfect gift. Teach me to give thanks in all circumstances, trusting in Your sovereign plan for my life. May my gratitude overflow as a testimony to Your goodness and grace. In Jesus' name, amen.

DAY 321
FINDING STRENGTH IN VULNERABILITY:
OPENING UP TO GROWTH

Scripture: "But he said to me, 'My grace is sufficient for you, for my power is made perfect in weakness.' Therefore I will boast all the more gladly about my weaknesses, so that Christ's power may rest on me." - 2 Corinthians 12:9 (KJV)

Strength is not found in hiding your vulnerabilities, but in embracing them and allowing God's grace to work through your weaknesses. Just as Paul boasted in his weaknesses, so too can you find strength in vulnerability, for it is in acknowledging your limitations that you make room for God's power to work in your life. Open yourself up to growth by embracing vulnerability as a pathway to deeper intimacy with God and others. As you allow yourself to be transparent and authentic, you create space for healing, transformation, and divine intervention.

Prayer: Heavenly Father, help me to embrace vulnerability as a means of experiencing Your grace and power in my life. Give me the courage to open up to growth, knowing that You are faithful to work through my weaknesses. May Your strength be made perfect in my vulnerability. In Jesus' name, amen.

DAY 322
RESILIENCE IN THE FACE OF FEAR:
CONFRONTING CHALLENGES WITH COURAGE

Scripture: "Fear thou not; for I am with thee: be not dismayed; for I am thy God: I will strengthen thee; yea, I will help thee; yea, I will uphold thee with the right hand of my righteousness." - Isaiah 41:10 (KJV)

In the face of fear, remember that you are not alone. God promises to strengthen, help, and uphold you with His righteous hand. Just as He reassured Joshua before entering the Promised Land, so too does He offer you courage and strength in the midst of life's challenges. Confront fear with faith, knowing that God's presence goes before you and His power is made perfect in your weakness. Trust in His promises, and step forward with confidence, knowing that He who is in you is greater than any fear you may face.

Prayer: Gracious God, when fear threatens to overwhelm me, help me to remember Your promise to be with me always. Give me the courage to confront challenges with faith, knowing that You are my strength and my help. Uphold me with Your righteous hand, and guide me through every trial. In Jesus' name, amen.

DAY 323
EMBRACING CHANGE: EMBRACING THE SEASONS OF LIFE

Scripture: "To everything there is a season, and a time to every purpose under the heaven." - Ecclesiastes 3:1 (KJV)

Change is an inevitable part of life, but it is also a sign of growth and transformation. Just as the seasons change, so too must you embrace the ebb and flow of life's transitions. Trust in God's perfect timing and purpose for each season of your life. In times of change, anchor your faith in His unchanging character, knowing that He remains constant amidst life's fluctuations. Embrace change as an opportunity for growth, learning, and new beginnings.

Prayer: Heavenly Father, thank You for the ever-changing seasons of life, each with its own purpose and beauty. Help me to embrace change with faith and trust in Your perfect timing. Give me the wisdom to navigate transitions with grace and the courage to embrace new beginnings. May Your presence be my constant anchor in the midst of life's changes. In Jesus' name, amen.

DAY 324
CULTIVATING RESILIENT SPIRITS: NURTURING INNER PEACE AND SERENITY

Scripture: "Thou wilt keep him in perfect peace, whose mind is stayed on thee: because he trusteth in thee." - Isaiah 26:3 (KJV)

True peace is not found in external circumstances but in a steadfast trust in God. Just as Jesus calmed the stormy sea with a word, so too can He bring calm to the storms of your soul. Nurture inner peace and serenity by fixing your thoughts on God and trusting in His unfailing love and sovereignty. Surrender your worries and anxieties to Him, knowing that He cares for you deeply. As you abide in His presence, He will keep you in perfect peace.

Prayer: Gracious God, in a world filled with turmoil and unrest, grant me the gift of Your perfect peace. Help me to keep my mind stayed on You, trusting in Your wisdom and love. Quiet my restless spirit, and fill me with Your serenity. May Your peace guard my heart and mind in Christ Jesus. In Jesus' name, amen.

DAY 325
THE POWER OF RESILIENT HOPE: FINDING LIGHT IN DARK TIMES

Scripture: "Why art thou cast down, O my soul? and why art thou disquieted in me? hope thou in God: for I shall yet praise him for the help of his countenance." - Psalm 42:5 (KJV)

In the darkest of times, hold fast to hope, for it is the anchor of your soul. Just as the psalmist encouraged himself to hope in God, so too can you find strength and courage in the midst of despair. Choose to fix your eyes on the promises of God, knowing that He is faithful to fulfill His word. Though the night may be long, joy comes in the morning. Trust in the Lord's unfailing love and find hope in His steadfast presence.

Prayer: Heavenly Father, when darkness surrounds me, help me to hold fast to the hope that is found in You alone. Fill me with Your light and dispel the shadows of despair. Strengthen my faith, that I may trust in Your promises and praise You for the help of Your countenance. In Jesus' name, amen.

DAY 326
EMBRACING GRATITUDE: FINDING JOY IN EVERYDAY BLESSINGS

Scripture: "In everything give thanks: for this is the will of God in Christ Jesus concerning you." - 1 Thessalonians 5:18 (KJV)

Gratitude is the key to unlocking the fullness of joy in everyday life. Just as Paul encouraged the Thessalonians to give thanks in all circumstances, so too can you cultivate a heart of gratitude that overflows with joy. Take time to count your blessings and give thanks for the simple joys that fill each day. In moments of trial and hardship, choose to focus on the goodness of God and His faithfulness. As you cultivate a spirit of gratitude, you will find that joy becomes your constant companion.

Prayer: Gracious God, thank You for the countless blessings that You bestow upon me each day. Help me to cultivate a heart of gratitude, that I may find joy in every circumstance. May my life be a testimony to Your goodness and faithfulness. In Jesus' name, amen.

DAY 327
RESILIENCE IN THE JOURNEY: NAVIGATING LIFE'S TWISTS AND TURNS

Scripture: "Trust in the Lord with all thine heart; and lean not unto thine own understanding. In all thy ways acknowledge him, and he shall direct thy paths." - Proverbs 3:5-6 (KJV)

Life is a journey filled with twists and turns, but you are not alone in navigating its complexities. Just as the psalmist trusted in the Lord to guide his steps, so too can you place your trust in God's perfect plan for your life. Surrender your plans and desires to the Lord, acknowledging His wisdom and sovereignty in all things. Though the path may be uncertain, trust that He will direct your steps and lead you safely home. With faith as your compass, journey boldly into the unknown, knowing that God is with you every step of the way.

Prayer: Heavenly Father, as I journey through life's twists and turns, I place my trust in You to guide my steps. Help me to lean not on my own understanding, but to acknowledge Your wisdom in all things. Direct my paths according to Your perfect will, and lead me safely home. In Jesus' name, amen.

DAY 328
EMBRACING RESILIENCE: HARNESSING STRENGTH IN ADVERSITY

Scripture: "I can do all things through Christ which strengthened me." - Philippians 4:13 (KJV)

In the face of adversity, draw strength from the One who is greater than any challenge you may face. Just as Paul found strength in Christ to endure hardship, so too can you harness His power to overcome every obstacle. Choose to face adversity with courage and resilience, knowing that God's strength is made perfect in your weakness. Lean on Him for support, and trust that He will equip you with everything you need to persevere. With Christ as your foundation, you can face any trial with confidence and hope.

Prayer: Gracious God, when adversity threatens to overwhelm me, remind me that I can do all things through Christ who strengthens me. Fill me with Your power and courage to face every challenge with resilience and faith. May Your strength be made perfect in my weakness. In Jesus' name, amen.

DAY 329

THE POWER OF CONNECTION: BUILDING SUPPORTIVE RELATIONSHIPS

Scripture: "Two are better than one; because they have a good reward for their labour. For if they fall, the one will lift up his fellow: but woe to him that is alone when he falleth; for he hath not another to help him up." - Ecclesiastes 4:9-10 (KJV)

You are not meant to journey through life alone. Just as God created Adam and Eve to be companions and helpers to one another, so too has He designed you for community and connection. Nurture supportive relationships with others, where you can encourage and uplift one another in times of need. Be willing to offer a helping hand to those who stumble, knowing that you too may need assistance along the way. Together, you can weather life's storms and celebrate its joys as a community of faith.

Prayer: Heavenly Father, thank You for the gift of supportive relationships that help us navigate life's journey. Help me to build meaningful connections with others, where we can encourage and uplift one another in times of need. May our relationships reflect Your love and grace to the world. In Jesus' name, amen.

DAY 330

FINDING PURPOSE IN PAIN: TURNING CHALLENGES INTO OPPORTUNITIES

Scripture: "And we know that all things work together for good to them that love God, to them who are the called according to his purpose." - Romans 8:28 (KJV)

Even in the midst of pain and suffering, God is at work, weaving a beautiful tapestry of purpose and redemption. Just as Joseph recognized God's hand at work in the midst of his trials, so too can you find meaning and purpose in your pain. Trust that God can use even the most difficult circumstances for your good and His glory. As you surrender your pain to Him, He can transform it into a testimony of His faithfulness and grace. Embrace the opportunity to grow and learn through adversity, knowing that God is with you every step of the way.

Prayer: Gracious God, in the midst of pain and suffering, help me to trust in Your promise that all things work together for good. Give me the strength to surrender my challenges to You, knowing that You can use them for Your glory. May my life be a testimony to Your faithfulness and grace. In Jesus' name, amen.

DAY 331

RESILIENCE IN ACTION: TAKING STEPS TOWARDS PERSONAL GROWTH

Scripture: "But grow in grace, and in the knowledge of our Lord and Saviour Jesus Christ. To him be glory both now and for ever. Amen." - 2 Peter 3:18 (KJV)

Personal growth is a journey of continuous learning and development, fueled by grace and guided by the knowledge of our Lord Jesus Christ. Just as a tree grows stronger with each passing season, so too can you grow in faith and maturity as you walk with God. Take intentional steps towards personal growth by immersing yourself in the Word of God and seeking His wisdom in prayer. Allow His Spirit to cultivate virtues such as patience, kindness, and self-control within you. Embrace new opportunities for learning and serving, trusting that God is at work in every season of life.

Prayer: Heavenly Father, thank You for the opportunity to grow in grace and knowledge. Help me to take intentional steps towards personal growth, relying on Your strength and guidance every step of the way. May my life be a reflection of Your glory and grace. In Jesus' name, amen.

DAY 332
EMBRACING CHANGE: EMBRACING NEW BEGINNINGS

Scripture: "Behold, I will do a new thing; now it shall spring forth; shall ye not know it? I will even make a way in the wilderness, and rivers in the desert." - Isaiah 43:19 (KJV)

Change is not something to be feared but embraced as an opportunity for new beginnings. Just as God promised to do a new thing for His people, so too can you trust in His faithfulness to lead you into a bright and hopeful future. Embrace change with faith and courage, knowing that God is with you every step of the way. Release the grip of the past and open your heart to the possibilities of the future. Allow God to make a way where there seems to be no way, and watch as He transforms your life with His grace and power.

Prayer: Gracious God, as I face new beginnings, I place my trust in Your faithfulness and provision. Help me to embrace change with faith and courage, knowing that You are making a way for me. Guide me into the future You have prepared for me, and fill my heart with hope and expectancy. In Jesus' name, amen.

DAY 333

CULTIVATING RESILIENT SPIRITS: NURTURING INNER STRENGTH

Scripture: "I can do all things through Christ which strengtheneth me." - Philippians 4:13 (KJV)

Inner strength is not found in self-reliance but in Christ who strengthens you. Just as Paul found strength in Christ to endure every trial, so too can you draw upon His power to overcome every obstacle. Cultivate resilient spirits by abiding in Christ and relying on His strength. Surrender your weaknesses and limitations to Him, and allow His Spirit to work in and through you. As you lean on Him for support, you will find that His grace is sufficient for every need.

Prayer: Heavenly Father, thank You for the promise that I can do all things through Christ who strengthens me. Help me to cultivate a resilient spirit by abiding in You and relying on Your strength. May Your power be made perfect in my weakness, and Your grace be sufficient for every need. In Jesus' name, amen.

DAY 334

THE POWER OF RESILIENT HOPE: HOLDING ONTO FAITH IN DIFFICULT TIMES

Scripture: "Now the God of hope fill you with all joy and peace in believing, that ye may abound in hope, through the power of the Holy Ghost." - Romans 15:13 (KJV)

In the midst of difficult times, hold fast to the hope that is found in God. Just as Paul prayed for the Romans to abound in hope through the power of the Holy Spirit, so too can you trust in God's faithfulness to sustain you. Anchor your faith in the promises of God, knowing that He is faithful to fulfill His word. Choose to believe that He is working all things together for your good, even when circumstances seem bleak. As you abound in hope, you will find joy and peace that surpasses understanding.

Prayer: Gracious God, fill me with Your hope that surpasses understanding, even in the midst of difficult times. Help me to anchor my faith in Your promises, trusting in Your faithfulness to sustain me. May Your Holy Spirit empower me to abound in hope and experience the joy and peace that come from believing in You. In Jesus' name, amen.

DAY 335
EMBRACING GRATITUDE: FINDING BEAUTY IN EVERYDAY MOMENTS

Scripture: "In everything give thanks: for this is the will of God in Christ Jesus concerning you." - 1 Thessalonians 5:18 (KJV)

Gratitude is the key to unlocking the beauty in everyday moments. Just as Paul encouraged the Thessalonians to give thanks in all circumstances, so too can you cultivate a heart of gratitude that overflows with joy. Take time to count your blessings and give thanks for the simple joys that fill each day. In moments of trial and hardship, choose to focus on the goodness of God and His faithfulness. As you cultivate a spirit of gratitude, you will find that joy becomes your constant companion.

Prayer: Heavenly Father, thank You for the countless blessings that You bestow upon me each day. Help me to cultivate a heart of gratitude, that I may find beauty in every moment. May my life be a reflection of Your goodness and grace. In Jesus' name, amen.

DAY 336
RESILIENCE IN COMMUNITY: COMING TOGETHER IN TIMES OF NEED

Scripture: "Bear ye one another's burdens, and so fulfil the law of Christ." - Galatians 6:2 (KJV)

You are not meant to bear life's burdens alone but to share them with your brothers and sisters in Christ. Just as Paul urged the Galatians to bear one another's burdens, so too can you find strength and support in community. Reach out to others in times of need, and be willing to lend a helping hand to those who are struggling. By sharing each other's burdens, you fulfill the law of Christ and demonstrate His love to the world. Together, you can weather life's storms and celebrate its joys as a community of faith.

Prayer: Gracious God, thank You for the gift of community, where we can bear one another's burdens and share in each other's joys. Help me to be a source of strength and support to my brothers and sisters in Christ. May our relationships reflect Your love and grace to the world. In Jesus' name, amen.

DAY 337
EMBRACING VULNERABILITY: BUILDING AUTHENTIC CONNECTIONS

Scripture: "A friend loveth at all times, and a brother is born for adversity." - Proverbs 17:17 (KJV)

True friendships are built on authenticity and vulnerability, where you can share your joys and sorrows without fear of judgment. Just as Proverbs declares that a friend loves at all times, so too can you cultivate relationships where you can be your true self. Embrace vulnerability as a pathway to deeper intimacy with God and others. Share your struggles and triumphs openly, and allow others to do the same. In authentic connections, you will find strength, encouragement, and support to navigate life's journey.

Prayer: Heavenly Father, thank You for the gift of authentic connections that allow us to share our joys and sorrows with one another. Help me to embrace vulnerability as a means of experiencing deeper intimacy with You and others. May our relationships be a reflection of Your love and grace. In Jesus' name, amen.

DAY 338

THE STRENGTH OF RESILIENT HEARTS: OVERCOMING ADVERSITY WITH LOVE

Scripture: "And above all these things put on charity, which is the bond of perfectness." - Colossians 3:14 (KJV)

Love is the greatest weapon against adversity, for it overcomes every obstacle and binds hearts together in perfect unity. Just as Paul exhorted the Colossians to put on charity above all things, so too can you overcome adversity with love. Choose to respond to challenges with love and compassion, even when it is difficult. Let love be the guiding principle in all your interactions, and watch as it transforms hearts and lives. By embracing love, you will find strength to overcome every obstacle and shine the light of Christ in a dark world.

Prayer: Gracious God, fill my heart with Your love that overcomes every obstacle and binds hearts together in perfect unity. Help me to respond to adversity with love and compassion, reflecting Your grace and mercy to the world. May Your love be the guiding principle in all that I do. In Jesus' name, amen.

DAY 339
FINDING BALANCE IN CHAOS: NAVIGATING LIFE'S CHALLENGES WITH GRACE

Scripture: "Let your moderation be known unto all men. The Lord is at hand." - Philippians 4:5 (KJV)

In the midst of life's chaos, seek balance and moderation in all things. Just as Paul encouraged the Philippians to let their moderation be known to all, so too can you navigate life's challenges with grace and wisdom. Find balance by prioritizing what truly matters and setting healthy boundaries. Lean on the Lord for strength and guidance, knowing that He is near to help you in times of need. As you walk in moderation, you will find peace and stability amidst life's storms.

Prayer: Heavenly Father, help me to find balance in the midst of life's chaos, prioritizing what truly matters and setting healthy boundaries. Grant me the wisdom to navigate life's challenges with grace and moderation. May Your presence be my constant anchor, guiding me through every storm. In Jesus' name, amen.

DAY 340
RESILIENCE IN THE UNKNOWN: TRUSTING IN THE JOURNEY AHEAD

Scripture: "Trust in the Lord with all thine heart; and lean not unto thine own understanding. In all thy ways acknowledge him, and he shall direct thy paths." - Proverbs 3:5-6 (KJV)

In times of uncertainty, trust in the Lord to guide your steps and direct your path. Just as Proverbs admonishes to trust in the Lord with all your heart and lean not on your own understanding, so too can you find peace and confidence in His leading. Acknowledge God in all your ways, seeking His wisdom and guidance in every decision. Though the path ahead may be unknown, trust that He is faithful to lead you safely through. With Him as your guide, you can face the future with hope and expectancy.

Prayer: Gracious God, as I journey into the unknown, help me to trust in Your wisdom and guidance. Give me the courage to lean not on my own understanding, but to acknowledge You in all my ways. Direct my paths according to Your perfect will, and fill me with hope and expectancy for the journey ahead. In Jesus' name, amen.

DAY 341
EMBRACING CHANGE: FINDING STRENGTH IN ADAPTABILITY

Scripture: "For I am the Lord, I change not; therefore ye sons of Jacob are not consumed." - Malachi 3:6 (KJV)

Change is inevitable, but in God, there is stability and strength. Though circumstances may shift like sand, His character remains steadfast and unchanging. Just as the Israelites found assurance in God's immutability, so too can you draw strength from His consistency amidst life's transitions. Embrace change with faith and adaptability, knowing that God goes before you and walks beside you. Trust in His sovereignty to guide you through every season, and find comfort in His unchanging love and faithfulness. In the midst of uncertainty, anchor your soul in the Rock that never changes.

Prayer: Heavenly Father, in a world of constant change, You remain steadfast and unchanging. Help me to find strength and adaptability in Your unchanging character. Guide me through life's transitions, and grant me the faith to embrace change with courage and trust. In Jesus' name, amen.

DAY 342

CULTIVATING RESILIENT MINDS: FOSTERING MENTAL WELL-BEING

Scripture: "For God hath not given us the spirit of fear; but of power, and of love, and of a sound mind." - 2 Timothy 1:7 (KJV)

God desires for you to have a sound mind, free from fear and anxiety. Just as Paul encouraged Timothy to embrace the spirit of power, love, and a sound mind, so too can you cultivate mental well-being through faith and prayer. Nurture resilient minds by filling them with God's truth and promises. Guard your thoughts against negativity and doubt, and replace them with thoughts of faith and hope. Surrender your worries and anxieties to God, knowing that He cares for you deeply. As you cultivate a sound mind rooted in God's Word, you will experience peace and strength that surpasses understanding.

Prayer: Gracious God, thank You for the gift of a sound mind that comes from You. Help me to guard my thoughts against negativity and doubt, and to fill my mind with Your truth and promises. Grant me peace and strength as I trust in You to meet all my needs. In Jesus' name, amen.

DAY 343

THE POWER OF RESILIENT FAITH: TRUSTING IN DIVINE GUIDANCE

Scripture: "Trust in the Lord with all thine heart; and lean not unto thine own understanding. In all thy ways acknowledge him, and he shall direct thy paths." - Proverbs 3:5-6 (KJV)

Resilient faith is rooted in trust and dependence on God's divine guidance. Just as Proverbs admonishes to trust in the Lord with all your heart and lean not on your own understanding, so too can you find direction and purpose in His leading. Trust in God's wisdom and sovereignty to guide you through every decision and circumstance. Surrender your plans and desires to Him, acknowledging His lordship over your life. As you walk in obedience and faith, He will direct your paths and lead you into His perfect will.

Prayer: Heavenly Father, I acknowledge You as the source of wisdom and guidance in my life. Help me to trust in You with all my heart, and to lean not on my own understanding. Guide me in Your paths of righteousness, and grant me the faith to follow wherever You lead. In Jesus' name, amen.

DAY 344

EMBRACING RESILIENCE: RISING STRONGER AFTER SETBACKS

Scripture: "But they that wait upon the Lord shall renew their strength; they shall mount up with wings as eagles; they shall run, and not be weary; and they shall walk, and not faint." - Isaiah 40:31 (KJV)

In the face of setbacks, find strength and resilience in the Lord. Just as Isaiah declared that those who wait upon the Lord will renew their strength, so too can you rise stronger after every setback through faith and perseverance. Wait upon the Lord with patience and trust, knowing that He is working all things together for your good. Allow Him to renew your strength and restore your spirit, enabling you to soar on wings like eagles. As you persevere through trials, you will emerge stronger and more resilient than before.

Prayer: Gracious God, in times of setback and disappointment, help me to wait upon You with patience and trust. Renew my strength and restore my spirit, that I may rise stronger than before. Grant me the faith to persevere through trials, knowing that You are working all things together for my good. In Jesus' name, amen.

DAY 345
RESILIENCE IN RELATIONSHIPS: BUILDING STRONG BONDS THROUGH TRIALS

Scripture: "And let us consider one another to provoke unto love and to good works: Not forsaking the assembling of ourselves together, as the manner of some is; but exhorting one another: and so much the more, as ye see the day approaching." - Hebrews 10:24-25 (KJV)

In times of trial, strengthen your relationships by supporting and encouraging one another. Just as Hebrews encourages believers to provoke one another to love and good works, so too can you build strong bonds through shared experiences and mutual support. Come together in fellowship and unity, lifting each other up in prayer and encouragement. Bear one another's burdens and share in each other's joys, knowing that you are stronger together than apart. As you journey through trials together, you will deepen your bonds of love and friendship.

Prayer: Heavenly Father, thank You for the gift of relationships that strengthen and encourage us in times of trial. Help us to support and uplift one another, bearing each other's burdens and sharing in each other's joys. May our relationships reflect Your love and grace to the world. In Jesus' name, amen.

DAY 346

EMBRACING GRATITUDE: CULTIVATING THANKFULNESS IN ALL CIRCUMSTANCES

Scripture: "In everything give thanks: for this is the will of God in Christ Jesus concerning you." - 1 Thessalonians 5:18 (KJV)

Gratitude is a powerful antidote to adversity, for it shifts your focus from what you lack to what you have. Just as Paul encouraged the Thessalonians to give thanks in everything, so too can you cultivate a spirit of thankfulness in all circumstances. Choose to give thanks for the blessings that surround you, even in the midst of trials and difficulties. Train your heart to see God's goodness and faithfulness in every situation, and watch as gratitude transforms your perspective and attitude. As you cultivate a thankful heart, you will find joy and contentment that surpasses understanding.

Prayer: Gracious God, help me to cultivate a spirit of gratitude that overflows in every circumstance. Open my eyes to see Your goodness and faithfulness, even in the midst of trials and difficulties. May thankfulness be the melody of my heart, bringing joy and contentment to my soul. In Jesus' name, amen.

DAY 347
FINDING STRENGTH IN VULNERABILITY:
OPENING UP TO GROWTH

Scripture: "But he said unto me, My grace is sufficient for thee: for my strength is made perfect in weakness. Most gladly therefore will I rather glory in my infirmities, that the power of Christ may rest upon me." - 2 Corinthians 12:9 (KJV)

Strength is found in vulnerability, for it is in weakness that God's power is made perfect. Just as Paul gloried in his infirmities, so too can you embrace vulnerability as a pathway to growth and transformation. Open up your heart to God and others, allowing His grace to fill your weaknesses and shortcomings. Surrender your pride and self-sufficiency, and allow His strength to be made perfect in your weakness. As you embrace vulnerability, you will experience the power of Christ resting upon you, enabling you to grow and thrive in Him.

Prayer: Heavenly Father, thank You for Your grace that fills my weaknesses and shortcomings. Help me to embrace vulnerability as a pathway to growth and transformation. May Your power be made perfect in my weakness, and Your strength be my source of courage and resilience. In Jesus' name, amen.

DAY 348

RESILIENCE IN THE FACE OF FEAR:

CONFRONTING CHALLENGES WITH COURAGE

Scripture: "Fear thou not; for I am with thee: be not dismayed; for I am thy God: I will strengthen thee; yea, I will help thee; yea, I will uphold thee with the right hand of my righteousness." - Isaiah 41:10 (KJV)

In the face of fear, find courage and strength in the presence of God. Just as Isaiah reassured the Israelites of God's promise to strengthen and uphold them, so too can you confront challenges with confidence and trust. Do not be afraid, for God is with you wherever you go. Draw near to Him in prayer and meditation on His Word, and allow His presence to banish fear from your heart. With His strength and help, you can overcome every obstacle and face the future with courage and resolve.

Prayer: Gracious God, when fear threatens to overwhelm me, remind me of Your promise to be with me always. Strengthen and uphold me with Your righteous right hand, that I may confront challenges with courage and trust. May Your presence banish fear from my heart, and fill me with peace that surpasses understanding. In Jesus' name, amen.

DAY 349
EMBRACING CHANGE: EMBRACING THE SEASONS OF LIFE

Scripture: "To everything there is a season, and a time to every purpose under the heaven." - Ecclesiastes 3:1 (KJV)

Change is a natural part of life, for God has ordained seasons of growth, change, and renewal. Just as Ecclesiastes declares that to everything there is a season, so too can you embrace the ebb and flow of life with trust and acceptance. Recognize that each season of life serves a purpose in God's divine plan. Embrace change as an opportunity for growth and transformation, knowing that God is with you in every season. Whether you are sowing seeds of faith or reaping the harvest of blessings, trust in God's faithfulness to lead you through.

Prayer: Heavenly Father, thank You for the seasons of life that bring growth, change, and renewal. Help me to embrace change with trust and acceptance, knowing that You are with me in every season. Guide me through times of transition, and grant me the faith to follow wherever You lead. In Jesus' name, amen.

DAY 350
CULTIVATING RESILIENT SPIRITS: NURTURING INNER PEACE AND SERENITY

Scripture: "Peace I leave with you, my peace I give unto you: not as the world giveth, give I unto you. Let not your heart be troubled, neither let it be afraid." - John 14:27 (KJV)

True peace and serenity come from Jesus Christ, who offers a peace that surpasses understanding. Just as Jesus promised His disciples peace, so too can you cultivate resilient spirits by abiding in His presence and resting in His peace. Seek inner peace and serenity through prayer, meditation on God's Word, and communion with Him. Surrender your worries and anxieties to Jesus, and allow His peace to guard your heart and mind. As you abide in Him, you will experience a deep and abiding peace that transcends the chaos of this world.

Prayer: Gracious God, thank You for the peace that You offer, which surpasses all understanding. Help me to cultivate a resilient spirit by abiding in Your presence and resting in Your peace. Guard my heart and mind from worry and anxiety, and fill me with Your perfect peace. In Jesus' name, amen.

DAY 351

THE POWER OF RESILIENT HOPE: FINDING LIGHT IN DARK TIMES

Scripture: "Why art thou cast down, O my soul? and why art thou disquieted within me? hope thou in God: for I shall yet praise him, who is the health of my countenance, and my God." - Psalm 42:11 (KJV)

In the darkest of times, hope shines brightest. Just as the Psalmist questioned his soul's despair and encouraged it to hope in God, so too can you find light in the midst of darkness by placing your hope in Him. Even when circumstances seem bleak and despair threatens to overwhelm you, anchor your hope in the unchanging character of God. Trust in His promises and His faithfulness to see you through every trial and tribulation. As you fix your eyes on Him, you will find the strength and courage to persevere, knowing that He is the source of your hope and the light that guides your path.

Prayer: Heavenly Father, in times of darkness and despair, help me to anchor my hope in You. Give me the strength to trust in Your promises and Your faithfulness to see me through every trial. May Your light shine brightly in my heart, guiding me through the darkness. In Jesus' name, amen.

DAY 352

EMBRACING GRATITUDE: FINDING JOY IN EVERYDAY BLESSINGS

Scripture: "O give thanks unto the Lord; for he is good: for his mercy endureth for ever." - Psalm 136:1 (KJV)

Gratitude is the key to unlocking joy in everyday life. Just as the Psalmist exhorted to give thanks to the Lord for His goodness and enduring mercy, so too can you find joy in counting your blessings and expressing gratitude to God. Take time each day to reflect on the blessings that surround you, both big and small. Cultivate a heart of gratitude by acknowledging God's goodness and faithfulness in your life. As you give thanks to Him, you will find joy filling your heart and peace flooding your soul. Let gratitude be your constant companion, guiding you through life's ups and downs with a spirit of joy and thanksgiving.

Prayer: Gracious God, thank You for Your goodness and mercy that endure forever. Help me to cultivate a heart of gratitude, acknowledging Your blessings in my life each day. Fill me with joy as I give thanks to You, and may gratitude be the melody of my heart. In Jesus' name, amen.

DAY 353

RESILIENCE IN THE JOURNEY: NAVIGATING LIFE'S TWISTS AND TURNS

Scripture: "Trust in the Lord with all thine heart; and lean not unto thine own understanding. In all thy ways acknowledge him, and he shall direct thy paths." - Proverbs 3:5-6 (KJV)

Life is a journey filled with twists and turns, but God is the faithful guide who leads you every step of the way. Just as Proverbs admonishes to trust in the Lord with all your heart and lean not on your own understanding, so too can you navigate life's uncertainties with confidence and trust in Him. Surrender your plans and desires to God, acknowledging His sovereignty over your life. Trust in His wisdom and guidance to direct your paths, even when the way ahead seems unclear. As you walk in obedience and faith, He will lead you safely through every twist and turn, guiding you to your ultimate destination.

Prayer: Heavenly Father, thank You for Your faithful guidance in my life's journey. Help me to trust in You with all my heart, leaning not on my own understanding. Guide me in Your paths of righteousness, and grant me the faith to follow wherever You lead. In Jesus' name, amen.

DAY 354
EMBRACING RESILIENCE: HARNESSING
STRENGTH IN ADVERSITY

Scripture: "I can do all things through Christ which strengthened me." - Philippians 4:13 (KJV)

In the face of adversity, find strength and resilience in Christ. Just as Paul declared that he could do all things through Christ who strengthened him, so too can you harness the power of His strength to overcome every obstacle and trial. Draw near to Christ in prayer and meditation on His Word, and allow His strength to fill you. Surrender your weaknesses and limitations to Him, and watch as He equips you with the power to persevere through adversity. With Christ by your side, you can face any challenge with confidence and courage, knowing that His strength is made perfect in your weakness.

Prayer: Gracious God, thank You for the strength that You provide in times of adversity. Help me to rely on Your power to overcome every obstacle and trial. Fill me with Your strength, that I may face challenges with confidence and courage. In Jesus' name, amen.

DAY 355
THE POWER OF CONNECTION: BUILDING SUPPORTIVE RELATIONSHIPS

Scripture: "Two are better than one; because they have a good reward for their labour. For if they fall, the one will lift up his fellow: but woe to him that is alone when he falleth; for he hath not another to help him up." - Ecclesiastes 4:9-10 (KJV)

God designed us for connection and community, for together we are stronger. Just as Ecclesiastes declares that two are better than one and that a companion can lift up their fellow, so too can you build supportive relationships that strengthen and encourage you. Reach out to others in times of need, and be willing to lend a helping hand to those who are struggling. In community, you will find support, encouragement, and accountability to help you navigate life's challenges. Cultivate relationships built on love and mutual respect, and watch as they become a source of strength and blessing in your life.

Prayer: Heavenly Father, thank You for the gift of community and supportive relationships. Help me to build connections that strengthen and encourage me in my walk with You. May I be a source of support and blessing to others, as we journey together in faith. In Jesus' name, amen.

DAY 356

FINDING PURPOSE IN PAIN: TURNING CHALLENGES INTO OPPORTUNITIES

Scripture: "And we know that all things work together for good to them that love God, to them who are the called according to his purpose." - Romans 8:28 (KJV)

Even in the midst of pain and suffering, God can work all things together for your good. Just as Romans assures that all things work together for good to those who love God and are called according to His purpose, so too can you find purpose in the midst of your pain. Trust in God's sovereignty to bring beauty from ashes and turn your trials into opportunities for growth and transformation. Surrender your pain and suffering to Him, and allow Him to redeem it for His glory. As you walk in faith and obedience, you will discover that even the darkest moments of your life can be used by God to fulfill His purpose in you.

Prayer: Gracious God, thank You for Your promise to work all things together for my good. Help me to trust in Your sovereignty, even in the midst of pain and suffering. Redeem my trials and use them for Your glory, that Your purpose may be fulfilled in my life. In Jesus' name, amen.

DAY 357
RESILIENCE IN ACTION: TAKING STEPS
TOWARDS PERSONAL GROWTH

Scripture: "But grow in grace, and in the knowledge of our Lord and Saviour Jesus Christ. To him be glory both now and for ever. Amen." - 2 Peter 3:18 (KJV)

Personal growth is a journey of continuous learning and development, fueled by God's grace and knowledge. Just as Peter encourages believers to grow in grace and in the knowledge of Jesus Christ, so too can you take intentional steps towards personal growth and spiritual maturity. Commit yourself to lifelong learning and discipleship, seeking to deepen your relationship with God and grow in His likeness. Embrace opportunities for growth and transformation, and be willing to step out of your comfort zone to pursue God's calling on your life. As you walk in obedience and faith, you will experience the abundant life that Christ promises and become a beacon of hope and inspiration to those around you.

Prayer: Heavenly Father, thank You for the opportunity to grow in grace and in the knowledge of Your Son, Jesus Christ. Help me to take intentional steps towards personal growth and spiritual maturity, as I seek to deepen my relationship with You. Guide me in Your paths of righteousness, and grant me the courage to step out in faith. In Jesus' name, amen.

DAY 358
EMBRACING CHANGE: EMBRACING NEW BEGINNINGS

Scripture: "Behold, I will do a new thing; now it shall spring forth; shall ye not know it? I will even make a way in the wilderness, and rivers in the desert." - Isaiah 43:19 (KJV)

Change can be daunting, but it is often the gateway to new beginnings and fresh opportunities. Just as Isaiah prophesies that God will do a new thing and make a way in the wilderness, so too can you embrace change with hope and anticipation of the new beginnings it brings. Trust in God's promise to lead you through times of transition and change, knowing that He is working all things together for your good. Let go of the past and step forward with faith into the unknown, confident that God is making a way for you where there seems to be no way. As you embrace change with courage and trust, you will discover the blessings that await you on the other side.

Prayer: Gracious God, thank You for the promise of new beginnings and fresh opportunities. Help me to embrace change with courage and trust, knowing that You are making a way for me where there seems to be no way. Guide me through times of transition, and grant me the faith to step forward into Your perfect will. In Jesus' name, amen.

DAY 359

CULTIVATING RESILIENT SPIRITS: NURTURING INNER STRENGTH

Scripture: "But they that wait upon the Lord shall renew their strength; they shall mount up with wings as eagles; they shall run, and not be weary; and they shall walk, and not faint." - Isaiah 40:31 (KJV)

True strength comes from waiting upon the Lord and relying on His power. Just as Isaiah promises that those who wait upon the Lord will renew their strength, so too can you cultivate a resilient spirit by trusting in God's strength to sustain you. Wait upon the Lord with patience and faith, knowing that He is working all things together for your good. Surrender your weaknesses and limitations to Him, and allow His strength to fill you and empower you to face whatever challenges come your way. As you abide in Him, you will find that His strength is made perfect in your weakness, and you will be able to soar on wings like eagles.

Prayer: Heavenly Father, thank You for the promise to renew my strength as I wait upon You. Help me to cultivate a resilient spirit by trusting in Your power to sustain me. Fill me with Your strength, that I may soar on wings like eagles and run without growing weary. In Jesus' name, amen.

DAY 360

THE POWER OF RESILIENT HOPE: HOLDING ONTO FAITH IN DIFFICULT TIMES

Scripture: "And now abideth faith, hope, charity, these three; but the greatest of these is charity." - 1 Corinthians 13:13 (KJV)

Hope is the anchor of the soul, the steadfast assurance that God is faithful to His promises. Just as Corinthians affirms that faith, hope, and love abide, with the greatest of these being love, so too can you hold onto resilient hope in the midst of difficult times. Anchor your hope in God's unchanging character and His promises, knowing that He is faithful to fulfill His word. Even when circumstances seem bleak and despair threatens to overwhelm you, hold onto the hope that God is working all things together for your good. As you cling to resilient hope, you will find strength and courage to face whatever challenges come your way, confident that God is with you and will never leave you nor forsake you.

Prayer: Gracious God, thank You for the gift of resilient hope that anchors my soul in difficult times. Help me to hold onto faith in Your promises, knowing that You are faithful to fulfill Your word. Strengthen me with courage and perseverance, that I may face challenges with unwavering hope in You. In Jesus' name, amen.

DAY 361
EMBRACING GRATITUDE: FINDING BEAUTY IN EVERYDAY MOMENTS

Scripture: "In everything give thanks: for this is the will of God in Christ Jesus concerning you." - 1 Thessalonians 5:18 (KJV)

Gratitude transforms ordinary moments into extraordinary blessings. Just as Paul urged the Thessalonians to give thanks in everything, so too can you find beauty in everyday moments by cultivating a heart of gratitude. Pause and reflect on the blessings that surround you each day, from the warmth of the sun on your face to the laughter of loved ones. Even in the midst of challenges and difficulties, there is beauty to be found in the simple joys of life. Embrace gratitude as a way of life, and watch as it transforms your perspective, filling your heart with joy and contentment.

Prayer: Heavenly Father, thank You for the gift of everyday moments that fill our lives with beauty and blessings. Help us to cultivate a heart of gratitude, that we may find joy in even the simplest of pleasures. May our lives overflow with thanksgiving, glorifying You in all things. In Jesus' name, amen.

DAY 362

RESILIENCE IN COMMUNITY: COMING TOGETHER IN TIMES OF NEED

Scripture: "Bear ye one another's burdens, and so fulfil the law of Christ." - Galatians 6:2 (KJV)

Community is a source of strength and support in times of need. Just as Paul exhorted the Galatians to bear one another's burdens and fulfill the law of Christ, so too can you find resilience in coming together with others to support and uplift one another. Reach out to those around you who are struggling, offering a listening ear, a helping hand, or a word of encouragement. In community, burdens are shared, sorrows are comforted, and joys are multiplied. By bearing one another's burdens, you fulfill the law of Christ and demonstrate His love to the world.

Prayer: Gracious God, thank You for the gift of community, where we find strength and support in times of need. Help us to bear one another's burdens and demonstrate Your love to those around us. May our relationships be marked by compassion, empathy, and solidarity, reflecting Your love and grace. In Jesus' name, amen.

DAY 363
EMBRACING VULNERABILITY: BUILDING
AUTHENTIC CONNECTIONS

Scripture: "Confess your faults one to another, and pray one for another, that ye may be healed. The effectual fervent prayer of a righteous man availeth much." - James 5:16 (KJV)

Vulnerability is the pathway to authentic connections and healing. Just as James encourages believers to confess their faults to one another and pray for each other's healing, so too can you build meaningful relationships by opening up and sharing your struggles and triumphs. Embrace vulnerability as a strength, not a weakness, knowing that it is through our weaknesses that God's power is made perfect. Be willing to be real and transparent with others, trusting that God will use your vulnerability to deepen relationships and bring healing and wholeness to your life and the lives of those around you.

Prayer: Heavenly Father, thank You for the gift of authentic connections that bring healing and wholeness to our lives. Help us to embrace vulnerability as a strength, not a weakness, as we open up and share our struggles and triumphs with one another. May our relationships be marked by honesty, authenticity, and mutual support, reflecting Your love and grace. In Jesus' name, amen.

DAY 364

THE STRENGTH OF RESILIENT HEARTS:
OVERCOMING ADVERSITY WITH LOVE

Scripture: "And now abideth faith, hope, charity, these three; but the greatest of these is charity." - 1 Corinthians 13:13 (KJV)

Love is the greatest force in overcoming adversity and building resilient hearts. Just as Corinthians declares that faith, hope, and charity abide, with the greatest of these being love, so too can you overcome every challenge and trial by embracing the transformative power of love. Choose to respond to adversity with love, extending grace, forgiveness, and compassion to those around you. Love conquers fear, bridges divides, and brings healing and restoration to broken hearts and relationships. By letting love guide your actions and attitudes, you will find strength and resilience to face whatever comes your way, knowing that nothing can separate you from the love of God.

Prayer: Gracious God, thank You for the gift of love that overcomes every obstacle and adversity. Help us to embrace the transformative power of love, extending grace, forgiveness, and compassion to those around us. May our hearts be resilient in the face of trials, grounded in Your steadfast love. In Jesus' name, amen.

DAY 365

REFLECTIONS OF SERVICE: LOOKING BACK WITH GRATITUDE

Scripture: "I have shewed you all things, how that so labouring ye ought to support the weak, and to remember the words of the Lord Jesus, how he said, It is more blessed to give than to receive." - Acts 20:35 (KJV)

As you reflect on a year of service, may you be filled with gratitude for the opportunities to give and serve others. Just as Paul reminded the Ephesian elders of Jesus' words that it is more blessed to give than to receive, so too can you look back on your acts of service with gratitude and humility. Take time to remember the ways in which you have been able to support and uplift others, whether through acts of kindness, generosity, or compassion. Give thanks for the privilege of being able to make a difference in the lives of those around you, and commit yourself to continued service and ministry in the year ahead.

Prayer: Heavenly Father, as we look back on a year of service, we are filled with gratitude for the opportunities to give and serve others. Thank You for the privilege of being able to make a difference in the lives of those around us. May our hearts be continually stirred to love and good deeds, as we seek to follow the example of Your Son, Jesus Christ. In His name, we pray, amen.

CONCLUSION

As we close the pages of this daily devotional, we are reminded of the unwavering spirit that defines each member of our esteemed military family. These devotions, steeped in faith and resilience, have journeyed with you through the triumphs and trials of military life. Each reflection was a beacon of hope, a gentle whisper of encouragement, and a steadfast companion through the darkest nights and the brightest days.

In the stillness of the early morning, when the world is shrouded in the quiet before the dawn, it is your unwavering commitment to duty that rises with the sun. These moments of reflection have not just been words on a page but lifelines that tether you to a higher purpose, grounding you in faith amidst the chaos of the world.

For every step taken on foreign soil, every breath drawn in the face of uncertainty, and every sacrifice made far from home, your strength has been both tested and proven. This devotional has sought to fortify that strength, to remind you that you are never alone. The scriptures, prayers, and meditations within these pages have aimed to lift your spirits, offering a sanctuary of peace and a wellspring of hope.

As you close this book, carry with you the essence of its teachings. Let the wisdom gleaned from each devotion be your shield against despair, your sword against doubt. Remember the stories of valor and faith, and let them echo in your heart, inspiring you to press on, no matter the challenges you face.

Your journey is one of profound courage, a testament to the enduring power of faith. In moments of solitude, when the weight of the world feels unbearable, know that you are held by a divine strength greater than any earthly force. You are part of a legacy of warriors who have walked this path before you, fortified by the same spirit of devotion and resilience.

May the light of these devotions continue to guide your steps, may the prayers uplift your soul, and may you always find solace in the unyielding love and grace that surrounds you. Carry forward with the knowledge that you are cherished, your service is honoured, and your faith is a beacon that will lead you home. Amen.

GOD BLESS YOU!!

Made in the USA
Columbia, SC
17 June 2025

59500235R00178